We Can Change the World

We Can Change the World

Tales from a Generation's Quest for Peace and Justice

Douglas L. Murray

Ideas into Books®: W E S T V I E W
Kingston Springs, Tennessee

Ideas into Books®
WESTVIEW
P.O. Box 605
Kingston Springs, TN 37082
www.publishedbywestview.com

ISBN 978-1-62880-277-1

First edition, January 2024

The author gratefully acknowledges permission to reprint the copyrighted materials in this book: For information regarding photographs and quotations, see credits, beginning page161.

Digitally printed worldwide on acid free paper.

Dedication

To the legions of unknown and forgotten souls
who pursued their passion for a peaceful and just world,
and in that pursuit, drew us closer to its realization.

And to Charlotte—grow strong, live long, and change the world.

Acknowledgments

Historian Lauren Coodley, after reading early musings, was the first to urge me to pursue this project and offered important feedback throughout. Karen Brown of the Boulder Editors Group read the entire manuscript and offered important input all along the way. Bruce Erricson, Sharon Pastori, Don Macleay, Stevie Lamar, and Melinda Haas, read many of the essays and also offered encouragement and suggestions. Jeff Green provided invaluable archival research, but sadly succumbed to the pandemic before he could see this project come to fruition. Stephanie Grohs provided additional archival research. Rick Killion provided important insight into the challenging world of trade and hybrid publishing, as did Flynn Murray. David J. Smith was helpful in identifying and accessing the peace and justice community, an important audience for this project. Publisher Mary Catharine Nelson was a constant source of encouragement and advice. She made this book more than I had imagined. My wife, Robin Mitchell, has been an unflagging source of support throughout. Without her I could not have finished this project.

Table of Contents

We can change the world
rearrange the world
it's dying

if you believe in justice
it's dying

if you believe in freedom
it's dying

Graham Nash, "Chicago"

I. Prelude to a Quest

It is not taboo to fetch what is at risk of being left behind.

Akan proverb, Ghana

Somewhere along the way I became an old man. The indignities of age and infirmities that mark its passage crept up on me without warning. Still, I thrive. Perhaps, as some have said, I'm just a glass-half-full kind of guy. To that, others have responded: *A conflict in Europe threatening to go nuclear; an intractable slaughter of innocents in the Middle East; right-wing tribalists dismantling democracies at home and abroad; and the planet warming at a rate fast approaching, if not surpassing, the point of no return. You must be out of your frigging mind!*

I am not oblivious. Indeed, I remain acutely aware of those and other affronts to this most fragile of arrangements, the human endeavor. And while they are real and may even transcend all that has preceded, I am reminded that in some form, we have been here before. I am of that generation that learned in the fifties to "duck and cover" under grade-school desks in preparation for an impending nuclear blast. The vengeance visited upon peaceful civil rights marchers and the venomous defiance of white southern bigotry the televised backdrop to my youth; a fusillade cutting down young student protestors at Kent State my coming of age; and the plight of the impoverished billions across the Global South the canvas upon which my adulthood has been composed—I have born witness to it all. Still, as I look to the future, I am hopeful.

Why am I so seemingly sanguine? It's because I lived my life as one of those "other directed" souls, as David Riesman so presciently called us. In contrast to the American frontier myth of the self-made man, I unapologetically embraced the seekers who shaped, influenced, even defined me all along my journey. They pursued a vision of a better world built on peace and social justice, rejecting the mainstream conformity and its plastic, consumerist ethos that Riesman warned was taking over postwar America. I will be forever grateful they swept me up in their collective sojourn, and I believe they will yet prevail. In spite of the imposing sense of oncoming darkness, I am convinced they represent a foundation from which a brighter future will yet arise.

The tales that follow are of a quest shared with many intriguing and inspiring characters. We were always a minority among our generation; we were the exception that proved the rule. We came to define the postwar, baby boomer, children of the Sixties, protest generation. Sadly, in recent decades we have become increasingly characterized as anachronistic, as having largely disappeared after the end of the Vietnam War and the advent of the Reagan Revolution. We were a generational folly that dissolved into conventional careers and adopted middle-class ambitions, or so we are told. Yet in spite of the mainstream narrative, many of us embraced a range of causes and lifestyles, from civil rights and opposition to the Vietnam War to women's liberation, countercultural communes, solidarity movements, human rights campaigns, and more. Tens of thousands of us lived lives largely unrecognized but unflaggingly committed to building a more just and humane future. Even as we grow old, we continue that quest today.

Popular understanding of our generation's history is at times mired in lurid accounts of "sex, drugs, and rock and roll" from that singularly iconic decade known as the Sixties. In other instances, my generation is celebrated through the "great men" narrative of conventional historiography. The examples of John F. Kennedy and Martin Luther King, as transformative of our collective identity as they were, did not begin to illuminate the breadth and depth of the era through which we lived. A great many of our generation led lives largely unrecognized, beyond the glow of media limelight. They embraced a quest for peace and social justice but did so in the absence of notoriety and adulation. While they are not likely to appear in any future history book, their lives have in some ways been all the more noble for the obscurity in which they toiled. *We Can Change the World* seeks to revive a part of our history that remains mostly unacknowledged, and for those who did not live through it, unknown. It is a portrayal of everyday people living extraordinary lives.

I have written these tales as a memoirist. But as the narrative evolves I move from subject to medium, from my own journey as frame to the experiences of others as window, offering a view into this most remarkable era. It is a storyteller's progression from frontstage, to borrow from Irving Goffman, to backstage. While the stories follow linear time, they do so with a qualification. Einstein theorized that time moves through multidimensional space, bending and even folding back on itself. These stories likewise follow a temporal and spatial bending and folding, visiting, and revisiting periods and moments while coming at them from different angles.

Walter Benjamin observed that "history is written by the victors," which he forebodingly wrote as fascism overtook Germany's Weimar Republic prior to the Second World War. Today we see a disturbing resurgence of right-wing and authoritarian celebration of a history purged of everything from the Holocaust and racial injustice to women's struggles for reproductive rights. The history of our generation is being marginalized and trivialized, to be replaced with a renewed American triumphalism defined by a white, male vision of grievance-driven patriotism.

We Can Change the World is a reminder to my generation and those who followed that a great many lived lives guided by a moral compass of human decency, justice, and equality. Some succeeded, others failed, some continue on to this day, while still others made the ultimate sacrifice. This is a journey of optimism, a rejection of despair, even as some of these stories are more tragic than we might wish. My generation has persevered. My hope is that others will be moved to carry this quest forward to the realization of an even greater vision of a just, humane, and sustainable world.

II. The Napa Valley: A Time of Awakening

We have been molded by forces that surrounded us from birth. As we passed through childhood, parenting gave way to schoolmates and other influences that left their stamp on our character. Then teenage culture overwhelmed homespun family values as we became creatures totally foreign to the generations that preceded. Who we have become is far more a product of a social milieu than most are willing to acknowledge. In my case, my journey took shape in the rural reaches of a relatively small California town. While that experience had its idiosyncrasies, it was exemplary of a much wider swath of America from which many of my generation came.

The Napa Valley of the 1950s was as good as it gets. With a population of 15,000 to 20,000, Napa had all the benefits of a small town—good schools, little crime, you knew your neighbors. It was an hour from the San Francisco/Bay Area metropolis, yet for most in the valley the big city might as well have been on another continent. Napa, and its surrounding hinterlands, were the perfect place for a child, at least of a certain race and class, to grow into adulthood, swaddled in the reassuring security of televised cultural touchstones like *Leave it to Beaver* and *Walt Disney*.

But the same medium that celebrated 1950s Americana soon sowed the seeds of its demise. By the middle of the next decade, nightly images of lunch counter sit-ins, violent mobs, and snarling police dogs unleashed on peaceful demonstrators began to invade our small-town idyll. In rapid succession an array of assaults descended on a faltering postwar narrative, jarring a generation from its cultural conformity. A countercultural wave that peaked with the 1967 Summer of Love merged with widespread resistance to the Vietnam War, including the nationally televised confrontations in August of 1968 at the Democratic National Convention in Chicago. The rise of women's liberation gave further impetus to a sense that radical, perhaps even revolutionary change, was afoot in the world.

While the events were seemingly far away, it was a time of awakening that touched most everyone across the land, not the least of which was this small-town boy as he grew into manhood. It was the beginning of my lifelong journey through an era of turmoil and change that defined me, as it did an entire generation. That momentous changes could reach into such a bucolic and insular community speaks volumes about the breadth and depth of the forces that buffeted America. Those forces were as much a part of traditional institutions like church, family, and community as they were their antithesis. The following stories, while on the surface appearing relatively personal, are in fact windows onto how many came to embrace our generation's pursuit of peace and social justice.

1. The Better Angels of Our Nature

The mystic chords of memory, stretching from every battlefield and patriot grave to every living heart and hearthstone all over this broad land, will yet swell the chorus of the Union, when again touched, as surely they will be, by the better angels of our nature.

Abraham Lincoln, March 4, 1861

My father grew up in a family of Southern Baptists. His parents were late nineteenth-century refugees from the violence of the Appalachian Kentucky hill country, escaping to Colorado where Dad was born and raised. Religion cast a pall across my father's sharecropper childhood, ruled over by a harsh and bitter matriarch. My parents married while still in their teens. Soon after they fled west, and never attended church again. So, I find it strange, in hindsight, that they were so adamant about their son being brought up in the church. But every Sunday, at least until I reached my rebellious teens, I went to services at the First Methodist Church of Napa. I attended Sunday school first thing in the morning and then joined the adults for the weekly sermon. It was a torture in boredom, a kind of weekly somnambulism through a largely forgotten dimension of my childhood.

Seated in a hard wooden pew, I was dressed in a sport coat and a white shirt, with a narrow black tie chafing my neck. Black leather dress shoes, worn only to church, pinched at my toes and wore blisters on my heels. My mind wandered elsewhere as the pastor held forth, until my attention was abruptly snapped back to the moment when the adults on either side reached for the hymnals or Bibles at the back of the pew before us. I would rest the book in my lap, awkwardly waiting for someone to reach over and flip to the correct page. I moved my lips but was totally lost as to the meaning of the singing and recitation of prayers by the gathered faithful.

Then the pastor would launch into a sermon I rarely followed. The Reverend Andrew Juvinall was a tall, lean man who spoke in a deep baritone. His sermons, even if I could not grasp their intent, held my attention by their sheer sensory power. On one occasion I remember vividly, his sermon described Jesus bathing the feet of his disciples. As best as I could glean, he was saying that as Christians, it was our duty to wash the feet of our neighbors. Metaphors, allegories, and parables were way beyond me at that point in my childhood. All I recall thinking that day leaving church was—*Gross*! But over time, his sermons began to find their way into my restless young mind. He would often preach from the Book of Matthew, weaving between scripture and contemporary topics like "right-to-work laws," the anti-union initiatives against which he railed. He would expound upon the importance of the United Nations as a means of serving the poor or draw from the story of the Good Samaritan in the Book of Luke to extol the righteousness of the civil rights movement.

Reverend Juvinall's sermons stood in stark counterpoint to my grade-school lessons, which were entirely devoted to the celebration of the prevailing 1950s narrative of American exceptionalism. The storybooks, films, and field trips of my early schooling reinforced a vision that ours was a white, comfortable, and seemingly uniform society. Dinner table conversation assiduously avoided social issues as not fit for family conversation. Barbershop wisdom, which was offered up without solicitation during my monthly haircuts at Gene and Shirley's Barbershop, was essentially that the poor—primarily people of color—were lesser beings whose plight was the product of their own lack of effort and ability, perhaps even reflecting divine intent. Reverend Juvinall's sermons were my earliest memory of an alternative view of the controversies brewing in broader society, and this in the name of a Jesus most everyone in my community embraced, even as they drew decidedly different conclusions as to his message.

Years later, an Episcopal minister, Marvin Bowers, reflected back upon his experience during our shared time in Reverend Juvinall's church. "The First Methodist Church of Napa, where I was baptized and went to Sunday school, was a place where the social gospel was preached with courage and determination by the Rev. Andrew Juvinall. Andy's sermons, based largely on the Sermon on the Mount, called on us—even the teenagers—to put the teachings of our Lord into practice in the America of the 1950s. I grew up assuming that Jesus was in favor of civil rights, social justice, international cooperation, disarmament, and, certainly, feeding the hungry."

As the years went by, I discovered that Reverend Juvinall was a man unlike any I had known in my time in that quiet little community. His life both before and after I spent those few short years in his church is an odyssey worthy of the parables he preached.

After graduating from Northwestern University in 1928, Juvinall and a friend, Newton Nesmith, set out on a two-year journey around the world. Their adventure started in Amsterdam at the end of the 1928 Olympics. They bought a secondhand motorcycle with a sidecar and financed the trip by selling advertising in the form of a Shell Oil decal painted on the sidecar's panel. They set out south through Europe. Traveling into Northern Africa, they were the first to cross the Sinai Desert on a motorcycle. They carried a large roll of chicken wire on the back, which they spread across sand drifts that otherwise made the desert impassible. At one point when their motorcycle broke down, they lived in the desert with nomadic Bedouins for several months. The time spent among Arab Muslims deeply affected Juvinall, shaping his later embrace of a diversity of religions.

Newton Nesmith (in sidecar) and Andy Juvinall.

Juvinall and Nesmith Crossing the Sinai Desert.

When they reached a snowbound region of what is now Iran, they abandoned their motorcycle and found a rare airplane flight east. They navigated through parts of China's "no man's land," avoiding warring forces during an interlude in the civil war between Chinese Nationalists and the Red Army.

Along their journey, they met royalty and heads of state, including England's Prime Minister Ramsey MacDonald and King Alexander of Yugoslavia. But the most significant encounter of that epic journey came at the end of a two-thousand-mile detour to have a twenty-minute private audience with Mahatma Gandhi. It was a moment that had a profound impact upon the rest of Juvinall's life.

At the end of his world tour, Juvinall returned to Northwestern University, enrolling in the Garrett Biblical Institute in 1930. He graduated in 1932 with a degree in divinity. His first church posting soon followed in Savoy, Illinois. He embraced a "very liberal" interpretation of the Bible, according to his daughter. His vision of religion, shaped in part by his reverence for Gandhi, included the notion that all the great religions ought to be valued as having much to teach us, along with a passionate commitment to pacifism. But his embracing of what came to be known as the Social Gospel got him in considerable trouble, leading to his being asked to leave his first ministerial position.

But his beliefs and practices soon caught the eye of another proponent of the Social Gospel, James Baker, bishop over the California-Nevada Methodist Conference. Reverend Juvinall joined Baker and pursued his vision of Christian social activism through numerous posts over the ensuing half-century. In the early 1940s he visited the Japanese internment camps in Tule Lake and became an outspoken opponent of those wartime measures. He moved to Stockton soon after and worked to protect interned Japanese American farmers from land seizures and theft. At the end of the war, he developed community programs to help the returning internees get reestablished. Years later, when his son returned to Stockton to attend College of the Pacific, the Juvinall name evoked great respect among Japanese Americans, often leaving his son in the awkward position of not being allowed to pay for goods and services purchased from businesses of the former internees. Reverend Juvinall then spent an extended period in San Bruno in the 1950s before being reassigned to Napa in 1957. By the time he arrived at my church, he had already left a remarkable legacy throughout Central and Northern California.

Reverend Juvinall became an unassuming but powerful presence in the local community, eschewing deference for "Please call me Andy." He was well-known for his sense of humor. A seminary student who interned with Reverend Juvinall recalls a gathering of pastors with the bishop. Seated around a large table during a break, Juvinall offered in his deeply resonant voice that he had just read the Kinsey Report and learned that people who spent a significant part of their day thinking about sex had *paar haar*. With that unsolicited offering, he clearly had captured the attention of everyone in the room. The bishop looked down from the head of the table, his brow furrowing as he leaned in, and said, "What?"

"I said," responded Juvinall, "The report found that people who spent a significant time thinking about sex had," then raising his voice to a near shout, "poor hearing!" The bishop abruptly sat back in his chair and blinked several times, trying to stifle a laugh as his face shaded red. The other pastors also tried, mostly unsuccessfully, to maintain a pious demeanor, while Reverend Juvinall's booming laugh reverberated through the room. His sense of humor became a subject of frequent discussion according to the seminary student, sometimes the source of collegial appreciation, more often one of consternation among his pious brethren.

Not long after I stopped attending church, Reverend Juvinall, along with members of his congregation and others in the community, formed the Napa Race Relations Committee. On May 19, 1962, they took out a full-page ad in the local newspaper for what came to be known as the Open Housing Covenant. It read in part, "We hereby bear witness that we are ready to welcome into our neighborhoods residents of whatever race, creed or national origin." It included a small coupon that could be clipped, signed, and sent to the Methodist Church as a pledge of support. Over four hundred people returned the form.

His efforts garnered more than a little hostility. His family recalls a rash of threatening phone calls and letters during this period. A prominent West Coast "anticommunist" paper, the *Tocsin*, ran a front-page article claiming Reverend Juvinall was a well-known communist sympathizer and the Methodist Church Federation, of which he was an officer, was a front for the Soviet Union, a discredited claim from the McCarthy hearings several years earlier.

The hostilities culminated on September 9, 1962, when one of Reverend Juvinall's sons came home late at night to find a several-foot-tall white cross, with KKK painted in red letters, staked into the church parsonage lawn. The next day the *Napa Register* reported on the event. Rather than attributing the act to the Ku Klux Klan, the reporter observed, "It is unlikely that this group is responsible for placing the cross . . . more likely youngsters, or someone displeased with the Reverend's actions regarding race relations placed it there."

While the observation might have reassured some, the reporter ignored the dark history of the Klan in the Napa Valley, including several rallies, the last only thirty-seven years prior, with attendance exceeding ten thousand enthusiasts. Just as likely as youngsters, the cross could have been the work of those same rally attendees who had merely aged several decades but remained part of the community. Reverend Juvinall dismissed the event, making light of it with his typical good humor.

The following day, Frank Dunlap, a prominent attorney in Napa, returned home from a weekend away and found a second cross, identical to the first, staked in his front lawn. He lived outside of Napa far from Reverend Juvinall's home. He did not share Reverend Juvinall's views on the Open Housing Covenant. But his brother and law partner, John Dunlap, was a progressive voice in the community and outspoken supporter of the campaign. The second cross incident was clearly a case of mistaken identity. Frank Dunlap complained in the newspaper story that night, "This is not funny." John, on the other hand, told friends that his brother's being targeted for John's political views was a source of great and lasting amusement around their office and among the family. The combined cross incidents suggest a bit more initiative than what might be expected of youngsters out on a night's escapade, casting further doubts on the local reporter's assurances that the Klan was not involved. In addition, the mistake in identifying the intended target speaks to a lack of intellectual acuity not uncommon among Klansmen as well.

While Reverend Juvinall continued to enjoy significant support among a progressive element, the church membership began to decline. This was in part due to a larger trend among young people, including myself, of abandoning organized religion. But it was also a product of some in the community feeling decidedly uneasy with Reverend Juvinall's pursuit of a community living in harmony with racial and religious diversity.

He left Napa in 1964, about the same time I graduated high school. Once I moved away, I thought little about my years in the Methodist Church, or of Reverend Juvinall. But I later discovered he went on to embrace even bigger challenges than bringing the races together in my little hometown. He went to Mississippi as part of the 1964 Freedom Summer. He was one of several hundred volunteers, mostly white pastors, priests, and rabbis, who went from door to door with local Black organizers, registering Black voters long denied access to the ballot. The response of many of the southern whites was angry and at times violent, culminating with the murder of three volunteers outside of Philadelphia, Mississippi, by Klan members and the local police. The risk to volunteers was palpable throughout the Freedom Summer campaign.

Undeterred, Reverend Juvinall went on to Alabama, after the first march from Selma to Montgomery was driven back by police and white southern racists defiantly defending a segregated South. He marched in several subsequent demonstrations arm in arm with Black church leaders and activists, led by Martin Luther King, John Lewis, Ralph Abernathy, Coretta King, and Jesse Jackson, among others. Again, the pacifist protesters were met by angry white mobs. But the widely televised confrontations raised a worldwide outcry, leading directly to the adoption of the Voting Rights Act of 1965.

By 1966 Reverend Juvinall was back on the West Coast where he became pastor of the Hamilton Methodist Church in San Francisco. The church sat at the boundary of a largely Black community and the rapidly transforming Haight-Ashbury. In keeping with his past, he was once again in the middle of the social action about which he preached.

On Christmas Eve, 1966, the Hamilton Methodist Church held a free Christmas dinner sponsored by the Diggers, a radical group of community activists and street theater actors. Ralph Gleason, iconic San Francisco columnist, described the event as a "Christmas Eve for hippies." His article was the first reference in print to the San Francisco-based Diggers, who went on to foster a wide range of counterculture events and organizations, including the San Francisco Mime Troupe and the "Yippies." The evening sermon prior to the dinner, which fed over five hundred people, was titled, "Jesus Was an Outcast Beatnik," by the recently arrived Reverend Andrew Juvinall.

He became a widely recognized fixture in Haight-Ashbury, frequently seen striding down neighborhood streets at a pace few could match. He welcomed the community to the church gymnasium, which he soon converted into a youth center attended mostly by Black kids. It became a gathering place valued by both local youth and their working parents, who feared their children would fall prey to other outlets without the safe haven of the afterschool youth program.

He helped launch the Off Ramp, a coffee house and resource center to serve the dramatic influx of struggling young people in the Haight, the ugly and otherwise largely ignored underbelly of the 1967 Summer of Love. The church's efforts included providing food, counseling, medical clinics, and mental health services, all free to the local communities. As his "Christmas for Hippies" sermon had suggested, he sought to make his church an extension of the people he served. As a pastor who worked alongside Reverend Juvinall during that time observed, "Andy wanted people to understand that Jesus was a really good dude."

In keeping with his lifelong commitment to pacifism, Reverend Juvinall became an active presence in the antiwar movement, and the Hamilton Methodist Church a gathering place for those embracing the Social Gospel and the social action it called forth. He provided counseling and support for draft resisters and soldiers refusing to go to war.

Reverend Juvinall remained pastor of the Hamilton Methodist Church until he retired in 1971. He continued to participate in a wide range of social activism in San Francisco until he and his wife moved to Santa Rosa in 1975 to be closer to their children. There he became a driving force behind the Nuclear Freeze Initiative and organized tours to China, the Middle East, and elsewhere as part of his lifelong commitment to fostering understanding between nations, cultures, and religions. He died in January 1984 at the age of seventy-seven.

While I did not become active in the efforts for social justice for some years after leaving Reverend Juvinall's church, I recall being not only aware of but drawn to the civil rights movement at an early age. The calls for equal rights resonated somewhere deep within me while still a teen, putting me at odds in some cases with friends and family. I never embraced organized religion, neither in the time I spent in the Methodist Church nor in these subsequent six-plus decades, but some of Reverend Juvinall's teachings left a lasting, perhaps near-subliminal stamp on my conscience as I grew into a lifelong commitment to progressive social change.

From whence come our better angels, and what sets them to fly? Are we born with noble thoughts and motivations to serve greater causes than ourselves? Or are they nurtured and grown from fertile ground, as suggested in Matthew 13, the Parable of the Sower of seed? That is a debate I will leave for philosophers and theologians. But reflecting back on my childhood and early memories, I find it hard to explain the passions that arose within me so early in life in any other way but as a result of fortuitous encounters with positive influences. While I was not aware of the sweep of Reverend Juvinall's life, I found myself pondering the injustices of prejudice, discrimination, and segregation at a relatively early age, in no small part, I suspect, due to those somnambulant Sundays in his church.

Reverend Juvinall's house of worship was a far cry from my father's church. The Southern Baptists of Dad's childhood were an angry lot, worshipping a vengeful god. They were obsessed with the devil, hellfire, and damnation. Reverend Juvinall's church was about the good that came from serving humanity, particularly the poor. I am not sure my parents were entirely aware of the Reverend's teachings, but I suspect they were comforted that their son was not being raised in a church so dark as the one they fled.

The venomous religious beliefs that drove my father from his home seem to remain a powerful force in America today. I am left wondering if the cultural wars that rage across the land are, at least in part, little more than a playing out of that age-old conflict between the religion of an angry god of my father's childhood and the one Reverend Juvinall brought to my own. If the better angels of our nature are to prevail as President Lincoln assured over 150 years ago, there is still much work to be done by the Sowers of seed who follow in Reverend Juvinall's footsteps.

2. Scouts Honor and the Vietnam War

Tommy, bottom row left; Robby top row far left; Bruce top row next to Robby; author, top row far right; Jackie not pictured.

The Cub Scouts of America was a place where young boys began to internalize the values that defined what it meant to be an American. Rituals like the Scout Promise that "I will do my best to do my duty to God and my country" and the numerous mottos, salutes, and handshakes were a cornerstone of childhood socialization, as were the uniforms and ever-present Pledge of Allegiance. It all came together to reinforce a vision of an America to which we were unquestionably loyal and of which we were undeniably proud.

The Cub Scouts was also a place where boys developed a sense of belonging to a larger reality, where they bonded as part of "the pack," one of the earliest experiences of shared identity outside the immediate family.

America had come out of the Second World War as the industrial engine of the world economy. American triumphalism was everywhere in the mass media, from *Ozzie and Harriet* to Norman Rockwell's nostalgic cover illustrations for the *Saturday Evening Post.* Membership in the Scouts was where we laid claim to our part of the epic saga unfolding around us.

I joined the Cub Scouts in the mid-1950s at the age of eight. Pack 103 was made up of about a dozen kids from my third-grade class at Vichy Elementary School in the semirural region of northeast Napa. My father was Cub Scout Master for a time, as were a couple of the other dads. Several of the mothers, mine among them, served as Den Mothers who helped organize weekly meetings and group outings. It was an opportunity for parents to shape the character of their sons while strengthening the sense of community among rural and suburban families. We learned a variety of skills, many of them of marginal utility like knot tying or wood carving. We were regularly rewarded for a wide range of small achievements with badges, presented in formal ceremonies. But there were also more valued benefits such as joining the Fly League baseball team organized by our Cub Scout Pack. I was not one of the better players, but baseball came to occupy many of my summer evenings and, most importantly, it made me part of a team.

Still, my enthusiasm gradually waned. This was probably the earliest sign of what would become a lifelong character flaw, or so I was led to believe. I was not entirely at ease as a joiner. I found I was more comfortable with my own company. After a year or two of Cub Scouts I graduated to the Boy Scouts, but that lasted just long enough to go to my one and only Scout summer camp. There I honed my nascent skills as a marksman and won the camp championship on the shooting range, a talent I continued to sharpen over another decade but for which I eventually, and thankfully, found no further need. Soon thereafter I decided I had had enough of the pledges, uniforms, and martial rituals and gave up Scouting altogether.

Over the decades my sensibilities evolved into a combination of uneasiness with unquestioned authority, a cornerstone of what I understood as patriotism, and a realization that I was becoming a devout adherent to Marx's motto: "I don't want to belong to any club that would accept me as one of its members" (that was Groucho, of course, not Karl). The culture of duty and loyalty, still deeply engrained in me, became increasingly at odds with my growing curiosity and, more importantly, with my growing skepticism. As I emerged from adolescence, I was becoming ever more confused about what the world around me was about and where in that world I most belonged.

The 1960s was a time of rapid and profound change. The insular certainty of the 1950s gave way to the challenging of established conventions a decade later. By the latter half of the 1960s, the civil rights and counterculture movements began to converge with an anti-Vietnam War movement to create a heady brew of social and political turmoil. As a teenager I was influenced to some degree by the civil rights movement, but was otherwise largely oblivious to much of the countercultural trends. I was aware, as was everyone else, of the Vietnam War, but it seemed far away as I graduated from high school in 1964.

The military draft was changing all of that. It forced every young man of a certain age to at least contemplate what war might mean for our otherwise predictable life choices. For most of us, war remained a noble part of the American trope. It was part and parcel of America's destiny as the Leader of the Free World. War was a place where courage and character were forged and rewarded, à la Charlton Heston, Audie Murphy, and a range of other heroes of the Silver Screen.

Largely unbeknownst to me, several members of my Cub Scout pack were drafted or enlisted soon after high school. Once I moved away from home to attend college in the summer of 1966, I lost track of all of them. Then at the end of 1966 I got my first awakening. I had squandered my first semester at college. Partying and romance dominated my attention that fall and failing grades at year's end my just reward. The draft board wasted little time in calling me to task, and in January of 1967 I was summoned to the Oakland Induction Center. I was about to be drafted. My draft call was part of a massive increase in the number of draftees, roughly thirty-five thousand a month for the first three months of 1967, to meet the military buildup set in motion by the Johnson administration. I was not excited to go to Vietnam but was ready to do my duty as I had been taught.

The long line of young men being processed into the military that morning was a sight to behold. All of us stripped down to our underwear, most in white socks, white briefs, and white T-shirts. It looked like the casting call for Tom Cruise's scene in the movie *Risky Business*. Prior to reaching the station where vaccinations were given and where nervous recruits watched anxiously as those ahead of them were injected by a sinister-looking compressed-air gun, we first had to fill out a medical questionnaire. I assumed I had no ailments to report until I came to one box on the form that asked if I had had an ulcer. I checked yes. It wasn't much of an ulcer. It had been described to me as an irritation of the stomach lining that had caused me enough discomfort a few years earlier to see a doctor. Six months of antacid tablets and making peace with a disciplinarian father resulted in a follow-up X-ray showing no lasting effects. But I checked it anyway.

Each of us got back into line and presented the medical questionnaire to a doctor who stamped the form and then pointed the inductee to the vaccination line. Much to my surprise the doctor skimmed down my form, stopped, and circled the box I had checked. He instructed me to send in a doctor's report and told me to get dressed and leave. My relief at that moment came more from not having to get back into the vaccination line than any consideration of what it meant to pass one's physical and report for basic training. A couple weeks later my family doctor gave me a letter explaining the course of my medical condition, noting the ailment had persisted for a relatively short period of time and that I no longer had any trace of an ulcer. I sent it to the draft board assuming it would soon be time to get back into line and face the next phase of my life as a soldier. Instead, I received a temporary deferment in the mail.

The deferment system allowed individuals with medical conditions temporary or permanent exemption from military service. It also provided temporary exemption to anyone with a certain level of performance in school. Those two features helped explain why the armed forces in Vietnam were overly composed of people of color and the poor, as both lacked the financial resources to attend college and for similar reasons had limited medical histories. Meanwhile I became a much more diligent student. While the war remained ever-present, I went back to my normal life.

But the war intruded upon my world even as I continued as if it was not my affair. Six months after that visit to the induction center, my little Cub Scout pack came back into my life in an abrupt and tragic way. While home from school for the summer, an old friend called with sad news.

Tommy, one of the friendliest and funniest members of our pack, was killed in Vietnam just weeks after turning twenty, when he drove a truck over a landmine while working on a bridge construction crew. He had been drafted in late 1966, around the time I was called in for my induction physical. In a single moment the statistics and evening news accounts were brought home in a very personal way.

Tommy put a face on the war for me. I didn't even know he had gone to Vietnam. He had moved away from Napa at some point around the end of grade school. I had lost track of him, but a couple of my grade-school friends had stayed close. Tommy was a twin. His sister, Connie, I recall, was the most beautiful girl in our school. I have known other twins, and their relationships are often deeper and more complex than anything the rest of us singletons can possibly understand. I have heard losing a twin is likened to losing a limb. One is forever absentmindedly reaching for that missing appendage, only to be reminded painfully anew of that loss. I thought of Connie and how incomprehensible the depth of her suffering must have been.

Within a year a series of events profoundly altered my understanding of the war and soon irreversibly changed the way I would see and live in the world around me. In January of 1968 the Tet Offensive was launched by the North Vietnamese to spur the rest of Vietnam into open rebellion against the US occupation. The death toll of American soldiers, along with the Vietnamese on both sides of the conflict, rose dramatically. It was not lost on me that the soldiers on the front lines were largely drawn from that big increase in draftees a year earlier when I was called to the induction center.

Walter Cronkite, America's "avatar of objectivity," visited Saigon and then Hue just as the Tet Offensive began. When he returned, he produced an hour-long news report that ran after the evening news on February 28, 1968. At the end of his broadcast, he concluded that the United States was not likely to win the war but instead was in a stalemate to which the only honorable resolution could be a negotiated peace. His report dramatically undermined the existing narrative that the United States was winning once again in its eternal triumph of good over evil.

In March of 1968 the My Lai Massacre brought the country's attention to yet another reality of the war. Many of the victims, as is always the case, were civilians. Despite assurances to the contrary by people like General William Westmoreland, we increasingly came to understand that a significant portion of the Vietnamese casualties were innocents. Images of elderly peasants, young children, and others forcefully driven from their simple dwellings as their villages were set afire by American soldiers, part of an Orwellian "Pacification Campaign," told a very different story than one of heroic combat between US soldiers and a communist menace.

That fall I began to gain other insights into the war. Many of the young men who had been drafted after high school had either completed their tour of duty or were sent home early with combat wounds or other less visible but no less traumatic scars. While some had little or nothing to say about their time in war, others told stories that often stood in stark contrast to the official reports coming out of Washington.

My sense of the nobility of fighting for the Free World soon gave way to a growing revulsion over the war's senseless violence and even madness. I came to see it as a betrayal of everything I embraced as a child. The questioning that is part of normal coming-of-age merged with the gradual recognition of the deceit that was the war propaganda effort. It left me reeling. By late 1969 I had turned from passive observer to nascent activist as I began attending antiwar protests. It was during this time I learned about others from Pack 103.

Jackie came home in 1968. He had been drafted in late summer of 1966. Jackie was a happy guy with a great personality. He could convince you of anything. Sometimes, with a couple of others from our Cub Scout pack, we would fish the nearby creeks and explore the woods out in the rural reaches of the Napa Valley.

Jackie was the ace pitcher on our baseball team. His fast ball was nearly unhittable. That was in part because while it was fast, on some days it went everywhere but over the plate. In a day forever etched in my memory, Jackie plunked me with that fastball three times during an intersquad game. I was as slow getting out of the way as Jackie was fast getting that pitch to the plate, or at least somewhere in the vicinity.

When Jackie finished basic training he was assigned to a light infantry brigade, a unit comprised of combat soldiers but lacking artillery support. Sometimes referred to in military jargon as "the tip of the spear," they were to become the first wave of assault in combat situations.

Not long after arriving in Vietnam, Jackie found himself in the middle of a nighttime firefight. He climbed atop a fortified bunker to watch what he described as a fireworks show grander than any Fourth of July, a description reminiscent of the antiwar movie *Apocalypse Now.* Then an artillery round hit the bunker, throwing Jackie from the ramparts, and leaving him unconscious.

He came back with what was diagnosed as a concussion. He was in and out of Bay Area medical facilities over the ensuing several years with what was described only as a "serious disorder." The initial diagnosis of concussion would likely be one of traumatic brain injury in today's vernacular. His serious disorder was probably a progression of the initial condition to post-traumatic stress disorder (PTSD), which was closely associated with traumatic brain injuries seen in Iraq and Afghanistan veterans. But in the late 1960s the medical world was not yet prepared to comprehend the full extent of the wounds of the Vietnam War.

As had been said of many of my acquaintances, one of Jackie's friends observed, "Jack didn't seem the same when he came back. He wasn't the Jack I knew before 'Nam." Jackie soon slipped into substance abuse, yet another affliction overrepresented among returning veterans. He struggled with drugs and alcohol and became increasingly despondent. On July 15, 1973, some five years after his return, Jackie and a friend were target-practicing in a field on the southeast side of Napa. After firing all but two rounds from a 9mm pistol, Jackie fired a round into a nearby embankment. With the last round he turned the gun to his temple and pulled the trigger. He was twenty-seven years old.

In retelling Jackie's story to me years later, his basic training buddy reflected, "Jackie was a really nice guy. He did not belong in the infantry, and he didn't belong in Vietnam." While visiting my parents several weeks after I learned of Jackie's suicide, I told my dad about what had happened. Dad seemed at a loss for words initially, then mumbled something about how he had fond memories of Jackie from our Cub Scout days. His eyes filled with tears, and he abruptly turned and walked out of the room. I had never seen my dad cry, and I saw him break down like that only once after, when my mom died. I think he, too, was beginning to come to grips with the decay of that American ideal he had espoused as our Scout Master and continued to embrace until the reality of that war became undeniable. A proud veteran of the Second World War, my father's view of the Vietnam War changed no less dramatically than my own in the years after that war's end. During the same period, I learned of yet another member of Pack 103.

Robby and I were close friends throughout much of our childhood. We had great times exploring the rural woodlands around where we lived. I realized at an early age that Robby was fearless. More than once I had to consider whether our adventures were at the edge of or even beyond my somewhat more cautious sensibilities. While still in grade school we raced around on his stripped-down motorcycle, which was in no way street legal. After a couple of those harrowing rides, I became convinced if I was to ever see adulthood, I had best stick with my bicycle when hanging out with Robby. A bareback horse ride around his place one afternoon ended up with me planted face down in the dirt and Robby on top of me. He was laughing wildly while I was trying to get my breath and checking for broken bones, reinforcing my conviction that our childhood escapades involved greater risks than I was cut out for.

One of the last times we spent any significant time together was a couple of weeks at Scout summer camp. As is tradition, the last two days of camp were dedicated to a tournament in which individuals and teams competed in various events. I won the camp long gun marksmanship competition. The only other event I entered was an almost medieval competition with a nautical twist. It was called "canoe jousting." A two-man team was composed of one person with a paddle maneuvering the canoe from its stern as the other team member balanced at the bow of the ever-shifting canoe. The gladiator at the bow held a long pole, at the end of which was attached a boxing glove. The simple task was to bash the opposing team's combatant from the bow of their canoe into the frigid lake. I quickly picked up the paddle and Robby, just as quickly and with a wide grin, picked up the jousting pole. We went through seven or eight opposing teams in short order with Robby bludgeoning each challenger into the water. I merely had to keep maneuvering the canoe into the fray while Robby did the rest.

In high school Robby flourished. He was the captain of our league champion football team, and he was awarded All Conference honors his senior year. He was a defensive tackle known for playing with reckless abandon. When you got tackled by Robby, you knew it. The same year he was elected student body president. Robby seemed to be on his way. After graduating he went off to Colorado to play college football but returned home after a year with an injury that ended his football career. In late 1965 he enlisted in the army, somewhat predictably joining the Special Forces. He became a Green Beret.

Robby headed off to Vietnam in 1966 as an A-Team Medical Specialist. The details of his time there are sketchy, and he has adamantly declined to discuss them. But from family and friends I learned he went through repeated heavy combat. He was at one point the sole survivor of a combat unit during the Tet Offensive. He was involved in rescue and recovery missions where he saw closeup the horrors of war that few might comprehend. At one point Robby recalled in an interview with a stateside reporter that he came to question the whole purpose of his being there. He noted the Special Forces motto was *De oppresso liber:* "To free the oppressed." "I realized," Robby reflected, "we were the oppressor."

He returned home in 1968 as a highly decorated soldier. Once back in Napa he pursued a variety of careers, but his time in Vietnam continued to haunt him. He had near-nightly dreams of violence and of his own death, awakening in a cold sweat. During the day he had flashbacks to intense combat moments, leaving him disoriented and shaken. By his own account he became increasingly unstable. He was eventually diagnosed and treated for severe PTSD.

I reconnected with Robby very briefly at a high school reunion in 2004. As was typical of those gatherings, we had a quick embrace amid laughter and a promise to catch up at some point during the evening. We were then swept away in the sea of familiar faces. I did not see him again that night nor ever again.

Eventually, he left Napa and moved to a remote area near the Salton Sea. He changed his name and became a self-proclaimed recluse and "prepper," preparing for what remains unclear. He was seeking an isolated life to wipe out the memories of what he went through in war as well as the torment he endured during the years since. I did not have contact with him again until late 2020 when I began writing this book. A mutual friend sent a newspaper article to me about a fire that had destroyed a small town near the Salton Sea. The article described how the fire had swept through the small ranch Robby owned. He and his wife barely escaped but lost everything to the inferno. Several of us among his high school friends reached out to Robby to see if we could help and, in the process, pieced together a bit more of his life over these past decades.

He had built a wildlife sanctuary out of his desert retreat. Along with his wife, Satya, he continued to wrestle with challenges from the Vietnam War. She was one of only two members of her family to escape the brutal Pol Pot regime of the mid-1970s in neighboring Cambodia. She struggled with her own PTSD. They had found in each other the kind of support that so many others from that time and place had not.

One member of our little group that reached out to Robby convinced him to join the website created for our high school class. Robby did so and responded to the outpouring of well-wishers:

"After my life was disrupted by a horrific and classified journey, it took another tragedy almost fifty years later to bring me out of the brain fog. So, it seems that I have woken up in a reality with lots of warm memories of old friends that I have been out of contact with for a very long time."

Robby was clearly finding himself and it made me happy to reconnect with my childhood friend. In a recent phone conversation, it was fun to find him much as I had remembered. If the old expression, "larger than life and twice as sassy" ever applied, it was to Robby. I offered to share this book once it was done. He brusquely replied, "Write whatever you want. I don't care to read it. I just don't want to think about the Vietnam War ever again." Then, in closing, as if forgetting about his declaration just a moment before, he shared his continued anger over the loss of life, some to friendly fire, and over the misguided and misleading policies that put so many in harm's way. He signed off with some choice words, not to be repeated here, for Henry Kissinger and the architects of that tragic conflict.

Bruce was my best friend in grade school. Our families took summer vacations together, camping and fishing in the far northern part of California. Our parents would often get together on weekends for dinner and then play cards into the night. Bruce and I would retreat into his room where we would pour over books about World War II. We would regale each other with our knowledge of sea battles in the Atlantic theater, reciting battleship and cruiser armament, displacement, and speed, and speculate on whether one battle or another would have come out differently if a particular ship had been present. *Victory at Sea* was our favorite TV show. When C.S. Forester's *The Last Nine Days of the Bismarck* came out in 1959, we read it as soon as we could get our hands on it. Our childhood get-togethers were major geek fests.

As we went into high school we drifted apart. Bruce became studious, me not so much. He also became a serious long-distance runner. I would see him out on the country roads near where we lived, running seemingly all day long à la *Forrest Gump*. He was one of the best runners in the area. As time went by, he seemed increasingly drawn inward intellectually, and in pushing the limits of his physical endurance.

After high school, Bruce went off to Adams State College in Alamosa, Colorado. It is a school renowned for its national champion cross-country teams and Alamosa, at 7,500 feet elevation, is a mecca for endurance runners. The pinnacle of Bruce's running career came in August of 1968 when he finished forty-fourth in the Olympic Trials Marathon, one of only 113 out of 161 of America's best who finished the grueling twenty-six-mile race. He graduated with honors in January of 1969. Three months later, he was drafted.

Bruce volunteered for the Army Rangers to become a member of the elite Long Range Reconnaissance Patrol (LRRP). "Lurps," as they came to be known, were scouts dropped behind enemy lines to track troop movements. They often spent weeks alone or in small units in survival mode, enduring extreme conditions in the jungle while both following and evading enemy patrols. The choice seemed to fit Bruce's quiet, introverted demeanor, as well as his passion for pushing physical and psychological limits. At Fort Benning he trained in the humid, snake-, alligator-, and insect-infested swamps along the Georgia-Florida state line, at times spending weeks on end in the forbidding environs.

Then Bruce contracted pneumonia during one of his training missions and was hospitalized for an extended period. Upon his return to his unit, he was informed he would have to start Ranger School over again, and the time he spent hospitalized would be added to the end of his tour of duty. Bruce declined the conditions put on his return to the Rangers and was immediately transferred into the regular army. He was soon shipped to Vietnam and quickly found himself in combat.

When Bruce returned from the war, he went about his life as he had left it. He assiduously avoided any discussion of his military experience. His brother recalled Bruce once sitting down with their parents to tell them of his time in Vietnam. To his brother's knowledge, he never spoke of the war again. Some years later Bruce married. His wife recalls she "couldn't get him to talk about the war under any circumstances." But there were moments when she felt the war was weighing on him. The most she ever learned from him was an evening she asked if he had lost friends in Vietnam. To her surprise, Bruce began describing a firefight. He was in a foxhole as he witnessed friends taking fire around him and dying. His wife said she felt the pain behind his words and decided never to ask him about the war again. That moment became the exception that proved the rule of Bruce's unwillingness to share war-time experiences.

Bruce became a computer programmer in Silicon Valley, doing contract work for various companies, including Apple. He had a family and developed close friendships. His wife remembered him as a man "with a good heart," at peace with himself and a source of positivity to those around him. He never abandoned his passion for running. His wife recalled him sometimes getting up in the middle of the night, or on a morning when it was driving rain, and she would say, "You're not going out running now?" He would respond with an easy smile, "But this is a great time for a run," and off he would go for hours on end. Bruce died suddenly in 2019. He was seventy-two.

The Vietnam War was an end of innocence for my generation. For many of us it marked the abandonment of a belief system and set the foundation for what is central to who we became. The war was the beginning of an unending torment for some of those who came home. It has also been the source of unending sadness for the loved ones of those who did not. In the decades since the end of that conflict, I have come to realize that the Vietnam War lives on in so many of my friends. It has shaped my generation as perhaps only the Cold War threat of nuclear annihilation and the Kennedy assassination have in our collective memory.

To be clear, many came home to lead successful and fulfilling lives. Bruce was perhaps more indicative of many Vietnam vets than the others from my Cub Scout pack. He steadfastly eschewed discussion of his experiences in Vietnam. Whether he and many others were deeply traumatized, unfazed, or somewhere in between, we will never know for sure.

Some argue it was a just war and most remain proud of having served. I heard indirectly that at least one of my childhood acquaintances described his being drafted into the Vietnam War as the best thing that ever happened to him. Those of us who did not go to Vietnam can never fully comprehend how the Tommys, Jackies, Robbys, or Bruces of our generation experienced it.

The war nevertheless radicalized many of my generation, and I certainly count myself among them. Some of those whose lives became increasingly politicized were among the draftees and enlistees. But many more came from the ranks of American society that experienced the war from afar. The war drove us out of the idyll of our youth and the beliefs we embraced as children, forcing us to grapple with the disconnect between those beliefs and the harsh realities that descended upon our world. The acceleration of change that swept through the lives of the members of our little Cub Scout Pack 103 over the past half-century continues today, as my generation looks upon the present and ponders the future our grandchildren will inherit. Most of us share a common hope: that they will never face another Vietnam War.

3. Lil Sis and the Women's Health Movement

Chico Feminist Women's Health Center (CFWHC) directors - left to right - Judy, Dido, Clare, and Janet. Missing is the fifth director, Betty, the photographer.

The women's liberation movement was never about a handful of women whose names got remembered... It was sustained and shaped by a sea of women...

Anne Forer Pyne

Janet was an apparition, drifting on the edge of my senses. Sometimes she was there, more often not. Like an ethereal spirit, she was present but invisible at the same time. As I grew into adulthood, she changed. She became larger than life, not only to me, but to many others in her ever-expanding circle of empowered and powerful women. Then, seemingly just as I came to see her for who she truly was, she was gone.

We were raised in a home imbued with traditional values. As the elder male child, I was afforded the freedom to explore, experiment, and repeatedly reinvent myself. My little sister, in contrast, was kept sheltered. She was not allowed the luxury of disappearing like her brother for most of the day into the fields and woods around our rural home. Instead, she stayed close by and pursued activities in keeping with my parents', particularly my mother's, sense of propriety. Her sheltered youth was also a product of early health challenges that the medical profession now would describe as a compromised immune system. Extensive allergies and frequent respiratory illnesses kept her indoors. Yet I never heard her complain or even acknowledge her struggles.

We had our daily interactions, of course. But I mostly ignored her, even as I enjoyed the adoration an older brother came to expect from his younger sibling. As I moved through adolescence, I hardly recall my sister at all. She had her schoolmates as did I, and I assume her social life to match. But I never really paid any attention. The few times we had more extended interaction were on family camping trips where we were together constantly for days on end. But back home from vacations, my sister became a phantom once again.

By the time I was a senior in high school in 1963, I began to see my sister in a new light. Somewhere along the way, totally unbeknownst to me, she had developed a kind of quiet wisdom while I was careening through my teens. I would find myself at the breakfast table on a Saturday morning, a bit ragged around the edges from a night of carousing. As I hovered over a bowl of cereal, my mom would pass through the dining room, offering up a scowl and a head shake. Nothing said, but the disapproval was there for all to see. My sister would sit across the table with her placid, Gioconda smile, and offer some soft-spoken observation that invariably cut to the obvious. I remember years later likening those moments to what I imagined it would be like to grow up with Doctor Phil as my sibling, Janet's gentle but no less pithy comments reminiscent of his question about how something was working, while implying "or not." My sister had gone from invisible to very present, and it was annoying as hell.

After I went off to college, I saw Janet on home visits, but those occasions were again all about me, my grades, my classes, my friends, a recounting of all my college exploits. I graduated, then married two months later. I took a job in the state capital as a junior bureaucrat. The entire progression from grade school to career was fulfilling some ill-defined masterplan as I continued to occupy that hallowed place of pride and privilege in the family order. My sister remained mostly behind the scenes, quiet, kind, deferential when engaged, but otherwise hidden in the shadows. Hers was a childhood and youth worthy of a modern-day Jane Austen novel.

Janet went off to college in the late 1960s. Predictably, I suppose, she went to Chico State College, where I was just finishing my studies. She graduated several years later, and then, perhaps also predictably, she married and became a high school teacher. We were singing from the same hymnal.

Then my life began to go off the rails, at least from anything approximating the traditional middle-class aspirations of both our family and community of friends. I split with my wife, quit my job, grew my hair long, and began railing against "the system." From prized son to every parent's nightmare, I became a hippie radical.

My sister once observed that family dinners had gone from the dull and quiet affairs of our childhood to what she described as shouting matches between Lester Maddox (the segregationist governor of Alabama) and Abbie Hoffman (the fast-talking, wild-eyed leader of the Yippies). Neither my dad nor I were truly representative of those polarized caricatures, certainly not my dad. But he would carry on about my failure to appreciate what I had been given in life and I would in turn spout slogans from Karl Marx about how decadent and bourgeois our society had become. My sister would just listen quietly, my mom all the while scowling and shaking her head.

Since I had deeply disappointed my parents, my little sister, married and a schoolteacher, soon saw her stock rise in the family enterprise. But nothing lasts forever. Within a couple of years of my abandoning the All-American narrative and her promotion to celebrated bearer of the family crest, Janet quit her teaching job and soon after split with her husband. Then she came home for one of our semiannual family gatherings and declared she was a lesbian. That was a stunner for my parents, clearly beyond even my worst transgressions. I joked with my sister that first evening of our visit, "I bet they're back there in their bedroom tonight thinking, 'Ya know, that Karl Marx may not be such a bad guy after all.'" It was the beginning of a bonding that we had not known prior to our becoming the bane of our parents' existence.

In the ensuing years, I learned more about my sister's new life. She had become increasingly influenced by what came to be known as the second wave of feminism in the late 1960s, the first wave having been the women's suffrage movement at the end of the 19th and beginning of the 20th centuries. By the early 1970s, Janet was drawn to the women's health movement, which challenged the male-dominated medical profession's control over women's health, particularly control over women's reproductive decisions.

In 1970 less than eight percent of all physicians in the United States were women. Women's health issues, both reproductive and otherwise, were diagnosed and treated by men. Male biases were ever-present in the information women had access to and the prescriptive options they were presented. Young women were becoming more sexually active with the advent of the "sexual revolution." But they frequently found themselves being told by their male physicians that they were too young for birth control, should wait until they were married, and other advice reflecting prevailing gender-biased social norms. In contrast, those same male doctors invariably counseled sexually active young men like me to "be careful," offering little more than a professional wink and a nod to another prevailing social norm, namely that "boys will be boys."

By providing nonjudgmental advice and treatment for women from their peers, the women's health movement was a direct affront to the male-dominated medical profession of the time. In 1969, the same year the path-breaking Boston Women's Health Collective published *Our Bodies, Ourselves*, the Jane Collective in Chicago became a powerful advocate for free access to abortions, arguing for women's rights to make medical decisions affecting their own bodies. Then, in 1973, the ground upon which the women's health movement confronted inequality profoundly shifted, with the Roe vs. Wade Supreme Court decision and a California Supreme Court ruling lifting many state restrictions on abortion.

After abandoning her teaching career, Janet joined the Chico Feminist Women's Health Center in 1974. The Center had been initially organized as a self-help collective by a small group of women from a wide range of backgrounds, including field workers, waitresses, mothers, college students, and recent college graduates. Noticeably missing were medical professionals. It was an entirely lay worker approach to healthcare.

When Janet first applied for a Center staff position, she had yet to fully embrace the radical and socialist trends in feminism espoused by the organization's leadership. One of the directors recalled that Janet arrived for her interview in a pink gingham dress, long braids, and knee-length stockings. The interviewers glanced at each other with eyerolls and raised eyebrows. Janet's choice of the wholesome, small-town schoolmarm look was decidedly in contrast to the pants and "business casual" attire that was *de rigueur* among feminists determined to wrest workplace culture from its traditional gender-defined dress code. But they hired Janet as an entry-level staffer anyway, and she soon found herself developing a deep political and personal affinity with the staff and directorate. Within months, Janet split with her husband. Not long after, she embraced her newfound lesbian identity.

Abortions became a significant focus of the Center's work. Doctors were contracted from the Bay Area, as no local physicians would have anything to do with a feminist health clinic. It was the only such organization in Northern California, and there were none in surrounding states. Every Saturday morning the Center waiting room was packed with anxious and quietly desperate women, mostly poor and working class. The Center team performed intake interviews, basic medical evaluations, and counseling, all done by lay workers. The contract physicians performed thirty to fifty abortions during each Saturday's clinic. At the time, legal abortions were only allowed in the first trimester of pregnancy, so once the intake processing was completed, it took only a few minutes to complete the procedure. Very soon after opening, the Center was deluged by women from Oregon, Idaho, Nevada, and Northern California, seeking not only abortions but a wider range of healthcare and health education.

Much of the rest of the day-to-day work of the Center was focused on women's self-care, from teaching self-examinations to providing information on and access to effective but largely unpublicized self-help techniques, along with birth control, pap smears, hematocrit testing, and sexually transmitted disease screening. The Center provided a wide range of health services traditionally only accessible through a doctor's office. The staff and directors also underwent regular and extensive training with the assistance of local registered nurses supportive of the Center's mission. The Feminist Women's Health Center quickly became a dynamic and thriving alternative women's healthcare provider.

My sister threw herself into the work. She quickly moved from one of the twelve to fifteen staff members to one of the directors, and in the process became an integral part of the Center's leadership. The schedule was intense and the work all-consuming. Janet routinely worked ten- to twelve-hour days, six to seven days a week. In keeping with the Center's anti-professional vision, responsibilities were rotated regularly so all directors and some of the staff became proficient in all aspects of the Center's daily tasks.

With the rapid rise in the demand for the Center's services, staff and director salaries grew from marginal to relatively good, by local labor market standards. The Center used a sliding scale for fees based on ability to pay, and collected payment from both the state-funded Medi-Cal program and some private insurers. The Center became an appealing place of employment, particularly for non-college-educated women and those drawn to the political vision of the women's health movement. In keeping with the broader progressive culture of the time, decision-making was pursued through a combination of consensus-building and directorate leadership, which meant a considerable part of the management of the Center was done through frequent, long, and often intense meetings.

The Chico Feminist Women's Health Center became one of several such centers across the country, and quickly drew widespread attention. Janet began giving talks and participating in various local forums. Then, in 1977, she went on a national tour with two colleagues, visiting feminist women's health centers across the country, along with midwife groups and other organizations. She was the spokesperson for a demonstration in support of the Tallahassee Feminist Women's Health Center members on trial for entering a local hospital to protest predominant birthing practices. The hospital, like most medical facilities in the region, had been promoting Caesarian deliveries over natural births, a more profitable but potentially more hazardous practice at the time. The rate of Caesarian deliveries in the area was twice the national average. On another occasion she addressed the American Public Health Association Women's Caucus, to promote natural childbirth and greater reliance on midwives. Her passion for, and role in, the movement was growing rapidly.

The pushback to the movement was powerful. Chico was a relatively small town, and in spite of the presence of the college, the community was quite conservative. Some of the surrounding areas had long been home to extreme rightwing organizations like the John Birch Society. The county medical association and other professional groups constantly challenged the Center's legitimacy, on several occasions bringing lawsuits and other legal challenges. Frequent media reports, both locally and nationally, sought to discredit the Center, at times making inaccurate or entirely fictitious accounts of what the Center was about. Picketing and protesting occurred regularly around the Center facility. It was a time of both radical experimentation and powerful and even violent resistance, and my little sister was right in the thick of it.

When I went to visit Janet in her new life, I was struck by how she had become someone increasingly comfortable within herself—an identity she had forged largely during the years I was absent. She seemed alive and happy, embracing both the politics of feminism and her newfound identity. She had become a strong, steadying force in the local women's community. Colleagues described her as a calming influence in the pressure cooker that was the Feminist Women's Health Center. She was assertive, but not domineering. She was both articulate and persuasive in her beliefs. She particularly liked writing her thoughts down on paper, sharing her assessments and advice in long letters to her colleagues, friends, her brother, and even our parents—that latter endeavor reaping mixed results at best.

I learned more about the women's health movement each time we got together. Her thinking increasingly seemed to occupy a place at the intersection of class and patriarchy-focused feminism. While she was quick to point out the near-universal dominance of patriarchy in modern society, she had an almost instinctual commitment to empowering the poor and powerless. I had an intellectual appreciation of feminism and professed unqualified support for women's liberation. But my sister's life, her daily struggles, and her passion for women's control over their bodies, frequently challenged and gradually deepened my understanding of the struggle in which she was engaged. It was a time in which her slowly awakening sibling was not infrequently taken to task by others, on occasion in less than generous ways. But through it all, Janet maintained a loving and positive place in her life for her big brother.

Even as she flourished in her new self, her health suffered. Perhaps in part from the stress of living the all-consuming lifestyle of an activist, she grew increasingly fatigued and had decreasing periods of good health. For a time, she persevered. But after nearly six years on the frontlines of the women's health struggle, she finally left the Center in 1979 in an effort to revive her flagging health. She joined friends and former colleagues in the east Bay Area. There she found part-time work with foster children and engaged in labor activities with groups like Union WAGE (Women's Alliance to Gain Equality), walking picket lines, and other support work for nurses on strike at a local hospital.

But urban living soon began to further challenge her health. Air pollution and other assaults on her weakened immune system took an increasing toll. After several years in Oakland, she moved again, this time to Santa Fe, New Mexico. The high altitude and dry desert climate seemed to give her relief, and she began to feel renewed. She worked with disadvantaged individuals in the local community and became an advocate for people with disabilities, mediating on their behalf with government agencies and private entities like landlords and employers.

Several years into her new life in Santa Fe, Janet decided to have a child with her lesbian partner. Once again, my parents did not quite know how to respond. A grandchild sounded appealing, but how were they to handle this new twist in their daughter's already incomprehensible journey? After a few missteps, they began to warm to the idea. Within six months of my sister's decision, I discovered I was about to become a father as well. Soon both of us were new parents. When we visited the folks, the newborns quickly dispelled any doubts their grandparents still held. The fact neither of us were married, and my sister remained beyond anything my parents could quite grasp, the family tensions melted away in the glow of transgenerational bonding.

My sister and I grew closer, and we looked forward to spending more time together. The thought of our children growing up only six months apart in age further drew us into each other's worlds. Janet's relationship with her partner eventually unraveled, and several years later mine with my son's mother did as well. We both found ourselves in single-parent mode, fortunately in shared-parenting arrangements with our exes. I can only imagine our parents were hard-pressed to explain how their children's lives reflected the best efforts they had invested. Nothing they learned from their traditional American values could have prepared them for the journey upon which they now found themselves. Nevertheless, we had evolved into a place where the family seemed to find peace together, embracing whatever differences had arisen. My little sister was at the center of the healing and understanding that grew throughout those years.

But Janet's health problems, largely kept in check after she moved to Santa Fe, came back with a vengeance. She was diagnosed with breast cancer in 2002 and underwent an extended and difficult period of treatment. In spite of the debilitating effects of the disease and treatment, she continued to work. The sad irony of the times was that her marginal jobs, even as they reflected a noble commitment to helping women and the disadvantaged gain greater access to healthcare, left her with few options for accessing medical care for herself.

Janet's health improved for a time. She continued to work, travel some, and generally return to her normal life. But it became clear she had not won her battle. For the next two years I made regular visits, driving the six hours down to Santa Fe from my home in northern Colorado. Our kids were both growing into precocious young teens. I remember visits when my son would go into Janet's room and sit in a chair beside her bed for hours as she rested. They would talk and, in the process, they grew very close. She would not share their conversations, but often afterwards would comment on what a wonderful young man he was becoming. I had never felt so close to my sister as I did in those visits.

Gradually, I came to realize that my little sister was fading. Her treatments were increasingly ineffective, and her cancer spread. She reached a point where the inevitable seemed to be drawing near. We tried to make our visits more frequent and of longer duration. Then, soon after a Christmas visit in 2008, her condition declined rapidly, and late one afternoon she slipped into an unconsciousness from which she could not be roused. It was a bitterly cold January night, and a blizzard was blowing through Colorado. The freeway south to Santa Fe was impassable. The storm finally broke sometime in the early morning hours, and I was on the road before dawn. But I was too late. She died before I arrived, just weeks past her fifty-eighth birthday.

My sister's journey seemed far too short. But in time I came to realize we had finally found our way to becoming as close as siblings can be. Those last two decades with Janet left me grateful that she had remained committed to us throughout all those years, even as I was too self-absorbed for much of that time to carry my weight in our relationship. I suppose it is never too late, at least if one of the parties remains committed, to find one's way to that elusive place of closeness we all seek, but don't always find.

It would not be an exaggeration to say that the second wave of feminism allowed Janet to become who she really was and may not have become otherwise. Throwing herself so completely into the women's health movement was transformative. For me, it had a profound impact as well as I learned to see the world through my little sister's eyes. I watched her become an impassioned advocate for a world radically different from the one in which we were raised. In the process, I gained a deep and lasting connection with that annoying little kid who for so long dwelled in the hinterland of my consciousness.

People, most notably men, see women's liberation as a zero sum game in which each step toward greater equality is achieved through the loss of something valued. But reflecting back on my sister's journey and its convergence with my own, it would seem that what I gained came at the loss of mere illusion rather than anything of substance. What I gained was knowing my sister as an equal who became a powerful and positive force in my life. It cost me only the occasional dose of humility, something I have come to appreciate later in life as a gift. I will be forever indebted to my sister, and to the liberation movement that awakened her—and to no small degree me as well—in those last decades of her life.

4. When Martha Graham Crashed Fight Night

A speed bag purred with a seductive rhythm. A second labored nearby like a chugging locomotive. It was as easy to tell where the veteran honed his craft as it was the aspiring novice. A young boxer stood hunched into a heavy bag hanging in a far corner, snapping quick jabs and hard right crosses, followed by a left hook driven from a pivoting shoulder. *Pop-pop; Pop-pop, pow!* The heavy bag jumped and danced while the fighter circled to his left, bobbing, then slipping back to his right as he unleashed a powerful hook to the bag's midsection, followed by another that exploded from his crouching legs up through his body to the head of his imaginary opponent. *Boom!*

The whole scene was enveloped in the ever-present scent of sweat and staleness, seasoned with equal measures of rubbing liniments and Lysol. Immediately upon pushing through the gym door, one's senses were assaulted by the stringent odors and the fierce grunts of men waging violent combat, warning of the gauntlet awaiting within.

Fight clubs are the same everywhere, and I have dwelled in more than a few. Like Babe's Gym in East Oakland where I trained alongside an angry and sullen fighter known as "Snakebite." I never got in the ring with him, as the owner, Babe Figuera, once cautioned me, "Snakebite ain't kind to white boys from the suburbs." Or O'Leary's Gym upstairs over the Torch Club in downtown Sacramento, where I once went three rounds with Argentinian Enrique Jana, the fourth-ranked light welterweight in the world, as he prepared for his match with former champion Raul Rojas. I never laid a glove on him. Then there was "Newsboy" Joe Gavras's Action Gym in Napa, where I watched Mike Weaver train for his victorious heavyweight title bout with John Tate. By then I had grown wise enough to know that smaller guys didn't get in the ring with heavyweights, at least not twice.

I began boxing at Chico State College in the mid-1960s while still a teen. Boxing was, I thought, a natural fit for a kid who was moderately fast-of-hand and fleet-of-foot, but not big enough, nor strong enough, to excel in traditional sports like football or basketball. It was a time and place where young men were still expected to prove their manliness in whatever arena they might succeed. That most of us ultimately failed to acquit ourselves with distinction was irrelevant. You either aspired at one after another or suffered the consequences of social obscurity. Boxing was my last option as most of my peers had outgrown or outcompeted me years prior.

Chico was one of the last schools in the country to participate in collegiate boxing, along with Stanford University, the University of California, and the University of Nevada. Most others had dropped the sport, particularly after Charlie Mohr, fighting before a hometown crowd of ten thousand exuberant fans at the University of Wisconsin, fell into a coma and died soon after being knocked down in his 1960 national championship bout. But true to tradition, each January, at the beginning of the winter semester, a new class of would-be gladiators stepped into the ring to showcase their skills after spending the fall semester in Boxing 101. The annual fight night spectacle was the culmination of a grueling five month training.

Boxing was taught by Willie Simmons, a small, wiry man with a nose nearly flattened to his face, the wages of many years engaged in "the sweet science." He had sandy, graying hair, worn in a flat top shorn high and tight. He looked every bit the part of a boxing coach sent from central casting. Leaning over the top rope of the boxing ring with one foot resting on the bottom rope, his gravelly voice echoed through the expansive training room with its two practice rings and numerous punching bags lining the surrounding walls. His caustic chiding belied the affection he clearly held for his eager acolytes. "Willie's Bash," as fight night was known, was not the final exam for the course as everyone had already received their semester grade. It was, instead, a trial by fire from which new talent would be selected for the varsity boxing team that began its spring season in the weeks that followed.

Each match was a series of three, two-minute rounds, with the winner decided by three judges at fight's end. There were usually about fifteen bouts over an evening between fighters matched by weight and skill. The bouts of the January 1967 event began as scheduled, with most competitors staggering exhausted to the final bell. It was at the intermission that Willie's Bash took a turn from the decades-old tradition as provocative as it was unprecedented.

When the auditorium lights went up for the interlude, the ring master took the microphone and drew the crowd of 1,500 rowdy fans' attention to a lone young man standing up a roped-off corridor leading from the locker room to the ring. This was to be, the announcer bellowed, a special act for the evening's entertainment. The young man approached the ring with long graceful strides, stepping up the stairs and through the ropes like all the previous fighters. But unlike the others, he wore a tight-fitting leotard rather than the gym shorts and tank tops of the other fighters. He carried a large white ball, nearly three feet in diameter, commonly found in exercise classes.

I recognized him immediately, although I could not recall his name. He was one of the boxers I had sparred with repeatedly over the fall semester. He was shorter than me by an inch or more. He was thick through the chest, shoulders, and neck, with powerful arms. Our sparring matches were memorable, although perhaps as different experiences for each of us. While he was stronger, I had a longer reach and was faster. I jabbed him repeatedly while hovering just beyond his powerful, but ultimately futile, punches. As he grew frustrated he began swinging wildly. He caught me with one or two, but for the most part I slipped away. As he grew tired his defenses faltered. My jabs became sharper and increasingly accurate, with each strike more telling. I began to land harder right crosses behind my jabs. I could see his eyes watering and his nose reddened from the repeated blows. By the end of our sparring session his nose was bloodied, his brow and flesh around his eyes growing puffy.

He was back the next day, and the day after that. Each time we entered the ring I pummeled him until, mercifully, he was switched on to another opponent better matched to his skills. My attention shifted to my next adversary, and I did not remember seeing him again in the days leading up to the big event. But here he was, stepping through the ropes and into the center of the ring, back straight, head held majestically high, moving with confidence and grace.

Then music came over the public address system, filling the gym as he began to move. He took one, then another, leap across the ring, he kicked out in splits with the ball extended overhead. When he reached the far corner, he spun on one leg atop pointed toes, and repeated his leaping strides back to ring's center. There he dropped back onto the ball, lying with his back arched and one arm draped across his forehead casting an anguished gaze to the rafters above. After lingering there for a moment, he sprang back to his feet and circled the ring with the ball under one arm, staring intensely into the crowd with something between a noble and haughty gaze. He repeated various moves and poses until he closed his performance by placing the ball on the ring mat and spinning a full 360 degrees, stopping only to briefly rise up again on his toes, bowing ever so slightly with arms spread wide. His finale hinted more at contempt than gracious acknowledgment of his audience.

And for good reason. The crowd went from stunned silence as the performance began, to catcalls, growing in volume until it reached a boisterous rabble filled with homophobic slurs to which the young dancer appeared oblivious. He held forth for a full two minutes, the time normally occupied by a single round of boxing. When he finished, he walked with long, measured strides to the ropes, stepped through, then down the stairs, up the roped-off corridor, then disappeared out the exit, all the while besieged by a cascade of whistles and insults. I never saw or heard of him again.

My reaction to this whole spectacle was one of dismay and awkward embarrassment, but I did not make fun or cast aspersions like so many around me. I knew this guy. We had trained, fought, and bled together. What was he thinking, and who in hell encouraged him, or even allowed him, to subject himself to such humiliation.

Soon after, I learned the answer to at least that last question. It was Willie, the tough-as-nails boxing coach who, it turned out, had a second passion beyond fighting, and that was ballroom dancing. Somehow, Willie and this young man had come to an understanding that this was what my fight mate wanted. I assumed it was their agreed-upon fulfillment of the course requirements. Or perhaps it was Willie's way of allowing him to express what he had truly learned from his journey into, and back out of, "the manly art." That was, and remained, but one of many questions with which I was left after the evening's debacle.

I quickly forgot about the fighter-turned-dancer as my bout came not long after intermission. I fought with my usual style, sticking jabs, and moving outside the reach of my opponent. I won the first round handily. The second began as the first had ended with me remaining elusive and racking up points by striking without being struck. But midway through the round I was hit with a hard right cross. I staggered back into the ropes. As I sprang forward again my opponent hit me with an even harder punch. My knees buckled and I slumped backwards, the ropes the only thing keeping me upright. The referee stepped between us, looked into my eyes, which I recall were doing weird things other than focusing, and declared the fight over. That I did not go down, the traditional defining moment separating victor from vanquished, was little consolation. I lost by a technical knockout.

As the end of the '60s drew near, the context around me had changed. The growing counterculture movement, along with the civil rights, anti-war and women's liberation movements, were calling for a new social order, one based on peace, not violence. Many of my generation, not least of which was me, were reflecting on who we were, from whence we had come, and most importantly, who we wanted to become.

I decided boxing was taking a toll on me, both physically and psychically, and abjured further endeavor. By the time I quit fighting, both in and out of the ring, I had a broken nose, a damaged occipital lobe, a ruptured sinus, several broken teeth, a cracked rib (twice), and sundry other physical wounds. There were other scars, more psychic in nature, some I feared would linger long after the most visible damage had healed.

About the time I quit boxing I met a woman while spending a summer in Boston. She was a classical-trained pianist making her living as an accompanist for modern dance companies. She worked with Martha Graham, the granddame of modern dance, along with José Limón and other leading artists. At her invitation, I went to various performances and in the process, I came to know a few of the dancers and more importantly, gained an initiate's insight into the art form of modern dancing and the expressions of life it celebrated.

The movements in modern dance were both the telling of a story, and an expression of the artist's interpretation of the world through which he or she moved. Once I came to understand what modern dance was about, it became clear that I was experiencing theater at its finest, a harkening back to the silent movies that awoke generations a century ago to the sensual magic of physical storytelling. I was enthralled by it all.

Watching these masters of movement, I began to reflect back on that shocking, embarrassing, and until then, baffling moment on fight night nearly a decade gone. I began to realize my former boxing mate had been dancing out his struggles with the expectations of the times. His was a rejection of the brutality that had defined what it meant to be manly. In his exuberantly uninhibited movements, his leaping *grand jetés*, the spinning *pirouettes*, and the cheeky final *plié en pointe*, were a declaration of liberation, just as his anguished repose was a soulful mourning of the destructiveness of a toxic masculinity, which until that moment, we had shared.

I realized that I had arrived late to a larger dance that was the awakening of a new masculinity that was emerging from the 1960s. While beginning to embrace the touchstones of the countercultural and liberation movements of the time, I had remained entrenched in other dimensions of the socialization of my youth. Fighting and all the rest of primal manliness were still embedded in my psyche, as much as I imagined I had risen above them. It was my good fortune, perhaps in part due to that young man's liberatory defiance, that I began to reject many of the traditions that defined what I came to see as a dying culture of which I increasingly no longer felt a part.

I reflect back on that time in Chico, now a half century gone. I do so infrequently, but still, it comes to me. Ironically, I have little or no memory of the fighters I fought, nor the bouts I witnessed. But that nameless young man from time to time arises from my memories and gives me pause to ruminate on life's lessons. Of late, that fleeting moment of rebellion and liberation provokes a smile as I consider the importance to him, the continuing impact on me, and hopefully others, of that brave act of self-realization. I doubt he had any sense, or intent, of such a reach beyond himself at that moment. But reach he did.

It's funny how singular moments and brief encounters in one's life inform who we are and may yet become, at times even a half century later. Where boxing was generally considered a defining test of one's bravery back in my youth, in hindsight it now would appear the actions of that lone dancer in his rejection of tradition, and in such a spectacular way, was a greater act of bravery than all the rest of us achieved in our pummeling and punishing of each other in the ring.

I have no idea what became of him. I hope he found fulfillment in his life's journey. He surely made a statement not many others had made, and in my mind had earned the right to lay claim to victory in that moment. He had run the gauntlet and proven himself worthy, even if none of us could see it at the time. His was one more moment in an era of individual and collective rebellion, exploration, discovery, and liberation, and I am grateful I was a witness, and perhaps even a participant, in it.

5. Days of the Commune

The author and other protesters confronting police at the Earl Butz Republican Party fundraiser.

When my generation refers to "the Sixties," they are often describing an extended period that ran from the early 1960s into the mid-1970s, when various political movements in the United States reached their zenith and, in some cases, began to fracture into narrower identity-defined politics. The Vietnam War had come to an ignominious conclusion in 1975. Many of my generation who were radicalized by the war were finding new avenues to express opposition to an American reality decidedly in contrast to the myth of American exceptionalism. The war had become our primer for understanding the powerful role American foreign policy played in fostering global inequality. The civil rights and counterculture movements had a similar impact on our understanding of inequity and injustice within our own country. Young people were actively seeking alternative ways of being. Among them, "intentional communities" were one more opportunity to pursue peace and a more socially just world.

Political communes became a refuge from the anger and contempt progressive people encountered on a daily basis in American society. The rise of neo-conservatism and the Christian Right that heralded the coming of the Reagan Revolution fueled the vitriolic attacks on social activists. People who have endured the venomous fanaticism of the Right through the Trump era may not realize that America was also deeply divided through the 1960s and 1970s. When Ohio National Guardsmen unleashed a sixty-round fusillade on unarmed student protesters at Kent State in 1970, killing four, a national survey conducted soon after found that fifty-six percent of Americans found the Guardsmen justified in killing those young people. Labels like "dirty hippies" and "Godless communists" were attached to justifications and even celebrations of the killing of antiwar protesters. It was a time when being politically active required a significant tolerance for hostility, at times from within one's own circle of family and friends.

I joined the Mund Road Commune in early 1975. There were several communes in and around the Napa Valley during that time, and hundreds of others throughout California and the Northwest. Most were spiritual in nature or organized around a less well-defined desire to get "back to the earth." But the Mund Road Commune had a decidedly different bent, one more common to urban centers and larger university towns like Berkeley or Madison. This commune was all about politics, both personal and social. One could argue that back-to-the-earth or even spiritual communes were a political statement as well as both explicitly rejected mainstream norms and values. The primary difference, however, was that political communes were outward-looking, embracing political activism rather than the more inward pursuit of individual enlightenment and the celebration of self.

I was teaching at a satellite campus of Napa College in the upper valley town of St. Helena. I taught classes on contemporary political issues that drew mostly nontraditional students from diverse backgrounds. The classes became a venue to explore many of the tensions afoot in American society. Gradually, the classes gained notoriety among young people seeking insight into the processes of contemporary social change. While some were enrolled students, others were not, attending irregularly to discuss specific topics such as the labor movement, criminal justice reform, or the dynamics of the Cold War.

In late 1974 I found myself looking for a place to live. I had been living alone on a large estate on Diamond Mountain west of Calistoga as a caretaker. When the estate sold, I had to find new residence in short order. Learning of my plight, a couple of the students in my class invited me to dinner at their small communal-living compound in the foothills on the east side of the valley. During an enjoyable evening of conversation and exchange of ideas, they described a vision of a rather unique project they hoped to pursue. They envisioned a collective living effort devoted to providing support to a wide range of political initiatives in the Napa Valley and beyond.

Two of the men in the group had been politicized by the Vietnam War as I had, one having fled to Canada to avoid the draft, and both having become conscientious objectors. One of the men had lived in political communes in Montreal and San Francisco prior to returning home to the valley. He held a particularly strong commitment to both the political agenda of the Mund Road Commune and to exploring the alternative lifestyle that came with collective living. There also were those among the group who were drawn more to the alternative living traditions of the counterculture movement. But they, too, were intrigued with political activism to whatever degree it might fit with their countercultural sensibilities. With little further thought, I plunged into communal living.

The core of the group was composed of six adults, two of whom were single mothers with infant sons. In addition, there were another half-dozen adults and a couple of teenagers who drifted in and out of the commune for extended periods. While I was the oldest, nearly all of us were in our twenties. The three men among the core group lived in a barn converted into a bunk house, and the three women and two children lived in two small adjacent cottages. The more temporary residents lived either nearby and spent their days and evenings on the commune, or in campers and other less-permanent arrangements throughout the compound. The commune sat tucked away on a small rise in a wooded portion of a large ranch that was roughly a one square mile section, or about 640 acres.

In the period leading up to joining the commune, I had become increasingly active in what was described in those days as "radical politics." I had been frequenting a larger commune in Berkeley and was intrigued by how they were combining collective living and community activism. Once I moved into the Mund Road Commune, we began regular exchanges with our urban counterpart. Our small group attended demonstrations, speaker events, and other activities with the Berkeley activists in the Bay Area. In turn, members of the Berkeley commune came to participate in events we organized in the Napa Valley or visited just to escape the big city and experience the rural environment.

One of our initial activities involved an inmate support group that helped find jobs and create affinity networks for people coming up for parole through the California prison system. At one point Willie Tate of the San Quentin Six came to the commune, soon after completing his maximum sentence. Soft-spoken with an almost shy demeanor, he defied the image constructed by prison officials of a radical black militant bent on mayhem. In the little time he spent with us he appeared only to want peace.

Prison work was considered radical at the time. Today such efforts are quite mainstream, replete with corporate sponsorships, as recognition has grown of the racial and economic forces that underpin a penal system that at one point incarcerated nearly a quarter of all imprisoned people on the planet. But like so many of our efforts, prison reform was perceived as decidedly extreme for the times.

Several of our group worked seasonally in the vineyards of the wine industry, the largest employer in the upper valley. As a result, there was a well-developed support network for the United Farm Workers Union (UFW) within the commune. At one point UFW leader Cesar Chavez came to Napa to promote the union's organizing efforts. The commune took a key role in organizing and promoting the largest Napa Valley union event in recent history. Soon after, two of the members left for several weeks to work on a UFW organizing drive in nearby Yolo County. Those who remained behind provided financial support and took on other activities, particularly childcare, to allow two women from the commune to devote themselves full-time to the political initiative.

Perhaps the most notorious action undertaken by the group was organizing a protest demonstration outside of a Republican Party fundraising event held at Beringer Winery in St. Helena. The fundraiser was headlined by then-US Secretary of Agriculture Earl Butz. He was profoundly hostile to the labor movement in general, and the Butz-led Department of Agriculture was at the forefront of anti-union efforts targeting the UFW, along with efforts to dismantle New Deal agriculture policies and promote corporate agribusiness.

We worked for weeks organizing a demonstration that took place in the St. Helena City Park ideally located near the fundraising event. We went on local radio station talk shows and produced news stories for the local press drawing attention to the plight of low-paid farm workers and the impact of the administration's promotion of corporate agriculture on family farming. The transformation of the Napa Valley through the burgeoning wine industry was a problem of which longtime residents were relatively unaware. But corporate farming would soon become the defining feature of life in the upper valley and the source of some of its most intractable challenges.

On the day of Butz's fundraiser, a relatively large crowd, by local standards, gathered at the park. After various speeches the protesters marched to the winery, setting up a picket line in front of the event. After about thirty minutes the fundraiser was halted. Secretary Butz was escorted out a back road by his security detail, and a caravan of Lincolns, Cadillacs, and other "chariots of affluence" exited the winery's main gate. As police held open a path through the line of chanting picketers, the angry curses and gestures from red-faced donors became the high point of the day.

The commune provided support to other progressive activities such as maintaining a steady presence of picketers in front of car dealerships in Napa when the auto mechanics, ultimately unsuccessfully, tried to unionize the local shops. We soon found ourselves approached by mainstream political figures, including staff members of a state senator, a state assemblyman, and the head of the County Democratic Party, all seeking ways to link up with what they viewed as an emerging local political force. The Mund Road Commune was becoming a unique presence in the Napa Valley. It was evidence of the contradictory nature of the commune's efforts. We were viewed as radical and even dangerous by some in the community, and a source of much-needed alternative strategies for social problem-solving by others, a tension that predictably was never resolved.

In some ways the internal dynamics of the commune were more significant than the array of community political activities, certainly for the members of the extended group. We sought to equitably share the daily and weekly communal responsibilities. It may sound mundane in today's world, but cooking, housekeeping, tending to farm animals, and working in a large garden were all shared tasks among the group. We were not rigid as some folks preferred certain activities like working in the garden over other chores like shopping in town. The focus was on equitable distribution of the communal workload.

Perhaps more unusual was the pooling of income. This was made easier by the fact that all of us had relatively marginal incomes. My salary from teaching two courses each semester, rather than being a full-time faculty member, was fairly modest. Still, it had the benefit of being a steady source of income. Several others worked seasonally as farm laborers. Still others worked in local service jobs, and two of the group cut and sold firewood. Some further supplemented the communal income through unemployment benefits for various extended periods.

The rural economy of the mid-1970s allowed young people to live comfortably, albeit at a relatively basic level, on marginal incomes. The rent for our compound was roughly $125 a month, while food costs were low by present-day standards. We shared a single vehicle for transportation and had a second truck for the firewood business, so fuel costs were minimal. Several members, including two of the women, prided themselves on their mechanical skills, so vehicle maintenance was done entirely within the commune, further eliminating monthly costs.

To keep things running smoothly we conducted monthly meetings. While it might have appeared to be another rather mundane part of life in the commune, these meetings became some of the most intense, and ultimately revealing, dimensions of the whole experiment. The Saturday morning sessions typically began with updates on keeping the group financially solvent and also apprising members of various activities and upcoming events. But the meetings also became a place to better understand different perceptions of our shared existence. It soon became apparent that we experienced communal living and engagement with the world in distinctly different ways.

Over time the seemingly minor personal disagreements over things like domestic habits began to evolve into deeper discussions of class and gender. In particular, we found ourselves returning to class differences frequently. I learned a great deal about alternative perceptions of shared experiences that were shaped by growing up in different socioeconomic environments. I began to grasp how the limits on one's expectations and sense of what is possible were engrained in each of us at an early age. That socialization came to constrain some from taking steps others found relatively easy to embrace. Pursuing higher education, speaking in public, having a sense that one could do whatever one chose, were all profoundly shaped by the context individuals were born into, and class was at the heart of that context. Some of the group came from marginal working-class experiences while others were a product of upwardly mobile and middle class professional family backgrounds. Our universal truths came to be reinterpreted as class-conditioned perceptions.

Gender became the second resounding theme in these meetings. That theme eventually superseded class for some of us, for better and for worse. Exploring the beliefs into which we were socialized from an early age fostered a better understanding of, for example, women's work as double and triple duties. Domestic skills such as being a better cook or keeping a cleaner house, and the emotional skills of being more nurturing, a "good listener," or "naturally" better at child rearing were traditional truths that we came to deconstruct as being mostly learned behavior. That learned behavior in turn channeled individuals into roles which were awarded more or less value, both in broader society and also within the commune.

We began to recognize that the emerging "equality" for women in the workplace that some were celebrating did not necessarily come with a commensurate relief from more traditional roles, most notably in the domestic sphere. It was at least in part through these increasingly long monthly sessions that we came to recognize that so-called women's equality had, if we did not make major adjustments in other realms, added to the multiple shifts in a woman's daily life rather than freeing her from the limits of more traditional roles.

It was to a significant degree through our efforts at child-rearing within the commune that we began to come to grips with what it would take to really challenge the barriers traditional roles had placed on all of us. The two single mothers found it hard to participate in outside activities while raising young children. At first we thought sharing daily childcare would be enough to allow them to fully embrace the broader agenda of the commune. Each of the other members took one day a week to provide childcare for one of the children while the mother then worked outside the commune and engaged in political activities.

The added childcare indeed freed up one woman's time for broader engagement in the world. The second mother chose to retain her more traditional relationship with her son, a choice the group supported as well. But we soon came to realize that there were still basic activities that fell back on the child's mother which constrained her ability to engage outside the commune. She still had sole responsibility for tracking her son's weeks, months, and more. Did he have clean clothes to wear for the week, was he getting enough sleep, was he continuing to show emotional well-being? We concluded that a person providing eight hours of childcare was not enough to truly support a mother's pursuit of other experiences.

We expanded our support into communal co-parenting whereby each of us became responsible for weeks at a time for not just taking care of a child during set hours in a single day, but for planning and monitoring the child's well-being.

At the same time, we found our pooled income could be stretched beyond meeting living expenses. We began covering for one or more commune members to work full-time on organizing and other political activities. One of the single mothers joined the UFW union drive in nearby Yolo County as a full-time organizer. She was gone during the week and returned on weekends. While it was at times a difficult emotional adjustment for her (and notably not so much for her son), she soon concluded that it worked for both.

Among this group of young adults mostly isolated from the ideas proliferating on university campuses and within urban counterculture circles, the commune lifestyle was transformative. For a time, it felt as if we were living the alternative vision we hoped to foster through our broader community engagement.

The context of mid-1970s America was one of rapid and disparate change in progressive politics. Identity politics, always present in American culture, began to transcend broader agendas as the Vietnam War and civil rights movement gave way to solidarity movements with various national liberation and revolutionary struggles in the developing world. Black Power groups vied with church-based nonviolent organizations for leadership of the civil rights movement. Feminism grappled with liberal demands for better opportunity in the workplace versus a more militant separatist and antipatriarchal vison.

In the commune we increasingly found ourselves internalizing the broader social tensions. At the same time, we were becoming increasingly isolated from the upper valley community as we devoted ever-more intense efforts at working through our diverging ideas.

Feminism was a powerful force in the Left by that time, and it became increasingly important within the commune. Many of the women in the commune were gravitating toward a lifestyle that celebrated the absence of men in their daily lives. Some chose to continue to engage with men, at least those of us willing to work on the serious inequities that feminism challenged. Others were drawn to an ever-more radical feminism and began to withdraw from engagement with men altogether.

There was much left unresolved at the end of increasingly long and exhausting meetings. Rather than leave tensions to simmer until the next monthly meeting, we opted to hold additional sessions. While we found we were working through some of these difficult issues, we had less energy to carry on our work outside of the commune. Some of the groups we had been working with complained that we were less available to support activities in the valley than they had come to expect.

Meanwhile, our activism drew the attention of new actors and entities beyond the local community. Little more than a year into the commune's existence, we were approached by a representative of a Cuba solidarity group, the Venceremos Brigade. "The Brigade," as it was commonly referred to, was organizing its annual trip to Cuba and invited us to participate. The trip involved a month of construction work in a Cuban community, followed by an educational tour of the island. It was a means to protest the US economic blockade of Cuba and to contribute to alternative sources of information on what was happening in the Cuban Revolution. The invitation was an exciting opportunity to see firsthand what most Americans had been denied access to for nearly two decades.

The selection process for the Brigade involved interviews with all of the commune members who wanted to participate. From that process four members were invited—two of us from the original core group, and two from the broader transitory group. We had originally proposed that the commune make the selection from within our ranks. Instead, The Brigade organizers invited some of us while leaving others out. Among those not selected were key actors not only within the commune but in the broader political community.

We were faced with a dilemma: Should we demand that we decide who represented us or refuse to participate, or should we accept the organization's decision? Ultimately, the organizers held to their choices and our group acquiesced. But the competitive dynamic created by the selection process, and the appearance of a more privileged class background among those who were selected, further eroded the ties within the commune.

We went to Cuba in the spring of 1976 (see Chapter 6). Immediately upon our return, we were forced to come to terms with the fractious reality of the commune. One member who had been passed over in the selection process moved out of the commune while we were away. At the same time, those of us who went to Cuba were drawn to larger political agendas we learned about while participating in The Brigade. We also found ourselves less and less enthusiastic about the increasingly tense and conflictual environment within the commune.

In early 1977 I left the commune and moved to the Bay Area. I felt the need to develop a deeper understanding of the powerful political processes that I had been swept up in over the preceding decade. The years of intense activism combined with the experience of trying to live a more egalitarian lifestyle left me with not only incredibly valuable experiences but also persistent and troubling questions. It was time for me to explore new and different paths forward as I grew ever more passionate about the potential for building a just and peaceful world.

The internal tensions that eventually broke the commune apart were revealing. We could not live apart from broader society and hope to have an impact on the issues we sought to change. But engaged in that broader society, neither could we avoid reproducing some of the very dynamics that underpinned the social relations and political processes we challenged.

Commune members Betty and Ron find the compound in ruins decades after its end.

Each member of the commune experienced that time differently. Some remain disillusioned to this day about the entire enterprise. But for me it was a powerful attempt to live by ideals deeply contrary to mainstream society. It was a laboratory of social change in which I made a major investment and within which I thrived. It was an opportunity to "walk the talk" of the progressive and counterculture movements. In the days of the commune, now nearly a half century gone, I learned as many lessons from our mistakes as our successes. Both became a part of who I am and how to this day I move through this ever-changing world.

6. The Brigade

A line of howitzers fired in timed succession. Concussive waves rippled through the sunbaked macadam, lifting me off my feet and assaulting my senses. I was swept along in a sea of humanity one million strong. Before me were row upon row of children in their blue-and-white uniforms. Behind trailed a chanting throng of teachers, farmers, soldiers, and more. I was part of a small contingent occupying a privileged place near the front of the parading masses. We were two hundred North American radicals marching through the streets of Havana to the Plaza de la Revolución. The artillery salute marked the opening of Cuba's May Day celebration. It was 1976.

As we filed into the plaza, the national orchestra struck up a triumphal refrain from the nearby grandstands. I glanced up to a dais draped in brightly colored bunting. There, in a khaki-green uniform holding a solemn salute, was Fidel Castro. I nearly stumbled over the woman in front of me as she halted, gazing up in rapture at the Cuban prime minister. It was a rock-star moment, part of an intoxicating months-long immersion in the forbidden revolutionary crucible just ninety miles south of Miami. An experience both inspiring and unsettling, it ultimately left me with as many questions as answers as to the potential and limits of this path to social change.

The Venceremos Brigade was organized by the Students for a Democratic Society (SDS) in 1969, with several hundred American radicals, loosely defined, journeying to Cuba to work in the annual sugar cane harvest. The Brigade was a statement of solidarity with the Cuban Revolution and an act of defiance to the US-imposed blockade on travel to, trade with, and information from the "New Cuba." In the context of the highly censured coverage of the Vietnam War, there was a large audience in the US and elsewhere for firsthand accounts that were not filtered through official US channels. The Brigade became one of many efforts to break the blockade.

We had gone through several months of orientation conducted by brigade organizers involving twice-monthly meetings. We were encouraged to ask questions while in Cuba, but also warned not to confront our hosts with challenges that, at least in the view of the organizers, reflected sensibilities shaped by living in a society of relative affluence within the dominant world superpower that was the United States. In effect, we were told we were there to learn, not to teach. We were also cautioned about what to expect from our own government's reaction to the trip, as well as the threat of right-wing Cuban exiles capable of extreme acts against anyone appearing to support the revolution.

It was a cold and drizzly spring morning when we arrived by bus at the San Francisco International Airport. Several dozens of us had gathered at houses in Oakland the previous night and were collected before dawn. We would meet up with other groups from around the country either in the Mexico City airport or once we arrived in Havana. The excitement, mixed with more than a little apprehension, was palpable. As we deboarded the bus we were confronted with a picket line of airport workers about to go on strike. The line stretched along the sidewalk in front of the airport terminal. To enter, it appeared, we would have to cross a union picket line. Our first crisis and we had not even left town.

We all agreed that crossing a picket line was not an option. Solidarity with Cuba did not trump solidarity with the labor movement. The Brigade organizers quickly huddled with the strike captains inside the terminal. The next thing I knew, the picketers had disappeared. We were hustled through the terminal doors and as I looked over my shoulder the picket line closed ranks behind us. You had to give credit to the Old Left activists that had largely taken over responsibility in recent years for organizing The Brigade, their ties within the labor movement remained strong.

When our flight arrived in Mexico City, we moved quickly to a boarding area in an isolated part of the airport. At several points along the way we encountered people ostensibly waiting for other flights, who surreptitiously snapped photographs and gazed ominously at us as we passed. These were the agents we had been forewarned would be taking note of our journey and, in some cases, visiting us upon our return.

After many hours of waiting at a gate that had no ticket counter and no signs designating the airline or destination, we were directed down a flight of stairs, out onto the tarmac, then up a movable stairway into a waiting Cubana airliner. Our plane was a Russian-made Ilyushin, a mainstay of Cuban air travel. Once airborne, the music began, the Cuba Libres flowed, and we all began to cheer as the long day's journey gave way to the realization that we were actually on our way to that mysterious world into which most of America had been denied even a glimpse.

In a jovial mood one of the *brigadistas* sitting across the aisle from me leaned over and said loudly enough for all to hear, "You know why this plane is called the Ilyushin? It's because it's remaining airborne is mostly an illusion!"

We all laughed, enveloped in a spirit of revery, even if it felt a bit like gallows levity. As I glanced around, I noticed I was not the only one cinching my seatbelt tighter.

We were all acutely aware of the threats to Cuban-bound travelers leveled by Cuban exile organizations. Tragically, the warnings we received during orientation became reality just six months later when Havana-bound Cubana Flight 455 was blown out of the air by a bomb planted at the direction of two longtime CIA operatives, Luis Posada Carriles and Orlando Bosch, killing all seventy-three aboard, most of them teenage athletes returning from a competition in Central America. It remains the only midair bombing of a civilian airline in the history of the Western Hemisphere.

Once our flight arrived in Havana we were taken directly to a work camp in the community of Los Naranjos roughly an hour's bus ride from Havana, where we would remain for the majority of our stay. The camp was composed of several long, low barracks, each with rows of bunk beds and a communal shower. There was a central plaza with an amphitheater and another long, low building that served as a cafeteria.

Rather than working in the traditional sugar cane harvest, our brigade would be building a childcare center in a nearby community. The cane harvests had proven too difficult for North Americans unaccustomed to the hardships of tropical field labor. The choice of a childcare center was a stroke of genius. It highlighted the resources being devoted to empowering women, anticipating some of the debates over women's liberation running through the US Left. The Cubans clearly were light years ahead of the US and most of the rest of the world on this particular indicator of social progress.

The workday began at 5:00 a.m. Our alarm clock was a loudspeaker, placed right outside the barracks wall, little more than a foot from where my head rested on my bunk. Each morning it blasted the same song by popular Cuban singer Silvio Rodríguez, exploding to a pounding beat. By the second morning I found I was the first one out of the barracks in the predawn darkness. I would jump from my bunk before the first note, launched by the initial static and crackle of the record player needle hitting the vinyl disk. Within the week I was so anticipating the impending auditory assault that I was hopping from bed when I thought I heard the footsteps of the person walking across the plaza to the sound system room.

As a result, I was always one of the first in the cafeteria. At the entrance stood a long counter with dozens of white, two-ounce ceramic cups, filled with thick, black coffee laden with sugar, the famous Cuban *cafecita.* The taste was exquisite. While standing at the counter, I would grab one then another cup and toss them back like a cowboy draining shots of whiskey at the saloon bar in an old Western movie. Then I would get back in line and do it a second time. From there I moved on to the row of servers loading plates with fried eggs, tortillas, boiled yucca, black beans, and white rice (known to Cubans as *Moros y Cristianos*, or Moors and Christians). By the time I got to the dining table I was grinding my teeth from the caffeine and sugar rush. If I was to work through the long hot and humid days ahead, that was the necessary precursor. I needed to *arrancar la máquina* (jump-start the machine, meaning my heart), as one Cuban worker counseled me.

On the daily bus ride to and from the worksite, we were matched with a Cuban counterpart, mostly members of Cuban youth organizations. My travel companion, Vilma, was a striking nineteen-year-old university student with a sharp, angular nose, high cheekbones and piercing dark eyes. She appeared more Middle Eastern than Latin American. But once she spoke there was no mistake, she was pure *cubana.* She was studying engineering and intended to pursue a career. Like many of our Cuban colleagues, she was born not long before the overthrow of the Batista dictatorship. She had only known her country under the revolutionary regime. Hers was a life of opportunities which her parents could not imagine.

Our conversations were conditioned by my limited command of Spanish, or more accurately, my capacity to comprehend that singularly challenging dialect that was Cuban Spanish. Still, I learned a great deal about Cuban life from Vilma that I could not have gleaned from my extensive readings, orientations, and all the formal presentations that accompanied the trip. On our first day, she was quick to inform me she had a *novio*, no doubt a conditioned reflex to make sure our time together would be one of clearly defined solidarity. In English that would translate to boyfriend, but in the Cuban context it was something more significant. The expectation was they would soon marry. But unlike prerevolutionary Cuba, Vilma implied she felt no rush, despite expectations to the contrary. As we exchanged questions and impressions, I could tell she was weighing that and other decisions against her desire to explore her independence. It was but one example of my frequent encounters with tensions in Cuban society between tradition and an uncharted future of intriguing but as yet unknown potential.

We started early and ended by midafternoon, six days a week. The work mostly involved unskilled labor like moving gravel, cement, and other building materials around the construction site and helping the Cuban craftsmen. While the work was difficult, there was clearly a sense of a comradery as the young Cuban *brigadistas* were mostly doing this work for the first time, as were many of the American contingent.

After a few days we began to grow accustomed to the heat and humidity as the project took shape. Much of the construction involved framing foundations and pouring concrete. Once concrete panels were laid as flooring, the Cubans began framing walls, windows, and a roof. Each day seemed slow going, but gradually we saw the initial chaos of dirt, rebar, and gravel piles transform into what would become a multiroom facility with playground and a paved access street. With the transformation we began to feel a sense of pride and accomplishment as well.

On Saturdays work was cut short, with the group returning to the barracks by midday. Everyone would rest up before dinner, and then as dark settled in, the camp quickly became one big party. Salsa bands from Havana, some of them among the best-known groups in Latin America, would perform for the evening. The rum would flow, dancing began, and everyone cut loose. While this was something we all threw ourselves into, it was clear the Cubans were much more accustomed to this part of our cultural exchange. They knew how to throw a party.

Fraternizing between Cubans and Americans was discouraged. Still, there were more than a few romances kindled on those Saturday nights. There even became a running joke about a mango orchard that spread for several acres from the edge of the camp, with sideways glances and giggles on the Monday morning bus rides about who wandered off into *Mangolandia* (mango land). One of the more talented members of the US contingent entertained us while working by singing his original composition, "the Ballad of *Mangolandia*," usually not shared in the presence of The Brigade organizers.

Sundays became an opportunity to visit nearby examples of the progress being made in the New Cuba. We visited schools that integrated farming and traditional curricula. The secondary schools were fulltime residential programs, and in most cases produced not only their own food but generated surpluses distributed in surrounding communities. We visited local health clinics that provided free services far in advance of anything I had seen in Mexico and Central America, and probably beyond what I might find in poor rural communities back home.

Some evenings after work, representatives from various political organizations, particularly liberation movements from Africa, the Middle East, and Latin America, which were not allowed into the US, would visit the camp. Formal presentations were followed by small-group question and answer sessions. A visit by several high-ranking members of the Angolan People's Liberation Movement (MPLA) was particularly timely. In March, just prior to our departure, the *New York Times* and *Washington Post* ran stories about a contingent of Cuban soldiers who were captured after raping and pillaging their way through a rural Angolan community. According to the reports, the community held a trial, and a group of Angolan women who were victims of the attack, executed their assailants by firing squad, using the Cuban soldiers' own weapons. The *Times* noted it could not confirm the report, but by running it they created a sense of the story's veracity.

The news reports caused considerable consternation in the US among supporters of the Cuban Revolution and fed into the fracturing already underway within and between various political organizations. The MPLA representatives offered a detailed explanation of how the incident did not and could not have occurred. But the story continued to feed into a narrative about the Cuban presence in conflicts around the world. Two years later, John Stockwell, the CIA station chief in Southern Africa at the time and with whom I would repeatedly cross paths a decade later in Nicaragua, acknowledged that he fabricated the story and planted it through journalists working with the CIA. It was yet further evidence of how the Cold War era control of information and the spread of disinformation was distorting American understanding of events around the world.

Cuba's role in international affairs was perhaps the most impressive aspect of what I learned during my time in Cuba. The Cuban government sent thousands of doctors and medical personnel to impoverished African nations, in some cases becoming the entirety of the health services in hard-to-reach rural areas. Cuban military advisers, and in a few instances combat units, also were assisting a number of liberation movements in various parts of the world. This again was cast as Cuban intervention by the US and others, but to hear from representatives of those liberation movements, Cuba was a crucial resource in struggles to break free from colonial and neocolonial rule.

After the month-long construction work ended, The Brigade went on a tour of the island. We visited industrial complexes where innovative and more appropriate technologies were being developed, largely in response to the blockade and the lack of access to parts and equipment traditionally purchased from the US. While the impact of heavy Soviet subsidization cannot be overstated, there was little doubt that the Cubans were holding their own in spite of the efforts to stifle the country's economic development.

We also visited several historical sites. Playa Girón was the place where Cuban exiles, organized and financed by the CIA, launched a disastrous attempt to invade the island in April 1961. The Miami-based Cubans and their US advisers believed that once the invasion was underway, a large part of the Cuban population would rise up and join in the overthrow of the Castro-led regime. That the Cuban population largely mobilized *against* the attack spoke volumes about not only the delusional echo chamber within the exile community, but about the equally ill-informed intelligence community and in the Kennedy administration. The Bay of Pigs invasion, as it came to be known, was defeated in seventy-two hours, a major coup for Cuba's domestic and international image, and an equally significant blow to US international prestige.

I was struck during several site visits by the impressive investments made in the arts as part of the national education system. It helped explain why such art forms as dance, music, and graphic arts had become world renowned. Sports, particularly baseball and boxing, also were showcased and, again, Cuban teams were generally considered among the best amateur competitors in the world.

For the final week of our stay, we returned to Havana. Some of us had become weary of being stewarded from farms to factories, schools to clinics. We had reached our limit of structured visits. At times, I began to question whether some of the glowing accomplishments might be more Potemkin Village than everyday Cuban reality. In hindsight, it was more likely a case of Soviet largesse leading to ultra-modern projects that looked out of place in the Cuban countryside, projects of which the Cubans were understandably proud, rather than an attempt at deception.

Some of us struck out on our own in search of more unscripted encounters. Through a connection made by a brigade participant, we visited with Margaret Randall, an American writer living in exile in Havana. She held a near cultlike status among some in the US Left. She had been an activist in Mexico City with students organizing against the Mexican government's violence and repression of the late 1960s. On October 2, 1968, the Mexican military brutally cracked down on a large gathering of student protestors, killing or wounding more than a thousand. Randall went into hiding as activists were rounded up, many tortured and imprisoned, some never to be seen again. After three months in hiding, she escaped to Cuba where she had lived ever since.

A small group of us gathered in Randall's living room eager to pursue our as yet unanswered questions. Randall was in her late thirties, a serious but gracious host, clearly at ease with the unfiltered and rapid fire questions the group threw at her. She reaffirmed what we had heard and seen. The revolution had indeed accomplished impressive feats, all the more remarkable for the hardships under which they had been achieved.

But Randall then began to diverge from the narrative we had heard over the preceding month. She observed that the threat from the giant to the north that permeated Cuban society, and particularly its security apparatus, ran a risk of stifling future advances. The calls for a unified resistance to that threat at times reinforced old cultural and particularly gender biases that created barriers to further progress. Calls for greater civil liberties and tolerance of wider diversity were being countered by the demands that some advances needed to be subordinated to the day-to-day survival of the revolution. The question for the *brigadistas* gathered in her living room, and for Randall as well, was whether that subordination would turn into a means of perpetuating old oppressions. While she did not pretend to have the answers, her candid observations were as refreshing as they were unsettling.

That question was further reinforced for me a day later with a visit to an ice cream parlor, La Coppelia, in a small park in Havana's Vedado neighborhood. One could find ice cream that rivaled the best in the world while seated at an old lunch counter–style creamery. There were dozens upon dozens of tropical fruit and other flavors that were the best I had ever tasted. I sat atop an old fashioned vinyl-upholstered stool that swiveled 360 degrees, one of fifteen lining the counter.

A young Cuban man seated next to me struck up a conversation in surprisingly good English. "You are an American? What kind of ice cream are you having? You should try the passion fruit or mango. They are my favorites. Did you know Fidel personally ordered this ice cream parlor built?"

He was in his mid-twenties, perhaps a few years younger than me. He was dressed in a casual shirt and jeans, much like everyone else around us, suggesting he was just another urban youth of indistinguishable class and ethnicity.

Our small talk then drifted into more substantive realms. "What do you think of my country? What have you seen? Yes, we have indeed accomplished a great deal."

Then he looked over his shoulder for a moment, scanning the plaza behind us. When he returned his gaze to me, speaking more softly, he observed, "But there is much you will not see. There are things that are not as wonderful as you are being told."

"Like what?" I asked.

Again, glancing behind us, this time somewhat more furtively, he whispered, "I cannot talk more. People are watching. But you should know, we are not as free as we would like."

He nodded to the ice cream on the counter in front of me, "I hope you enjoy your ice cream, and your stay, but don't forget what I have said."

With that he walked away.

We had been told during our orientation period that we might be approached by everyday people, among whom would be the occasional dissident or malcontent. We were told not to engage with them. But the young man did not seem, in any way I could discern, different from the young people I had worked with over the previous weeks, people I had ridden with each day to and from camp or met in various visits around the country. Further, we had all become a bit frustrated with the lack of acknowledgment that projects or policies had any shortcomings, or whether there was any real discontent at all among the Cuban population. The encounter added to what was the beginning of a questioning that I mostly set aside for the rest of our stay, but which would not remain unattended for long.

The crowning finale of our trip was the May Day celebration, an annual event occurring in many countries around the world. But in Cuba it represented something more. This was the day to celebrate not only the triumph of the revolution over a US-backed dictatorship but to tout the continued successful defiance of the small island nation in the face of the unrelenting blockade. The event drew over a million people and clearly demonstrated a popular willingness to continue resisting outside pressures, significant as they were. I had never been in anything approaching such a massive celebratory event. It was an exhilarating finale to our trip.

Two days later we headed home. We were all exhausted and looking forward to getting back, even as we were a bit sad to say farewell to a place we likely would never return. Upon our arrival home, many of us quickly began sharing our experiences and impressions. We were in high demand, from radio talk shows to newspaper interviews, church, community speaking events, and more. In the process, I also began to reflect further on a nagging disquietude. Questions I did not ask and others that were not answered, became more unsettling. Back home, people were not shy about pursuing concerns and engaging in debate, forcing us out of our post-brigade glow. It soon became a time to dig deeper for answers to questions not answered and to better understand issues not resolved during my stay in Cuba.

In the months and then years that followed my visit to Cuba, I reflected frequently on the lessons the trip had offered. A shorter return visit to Havana some years later confirmed many of my initial impressions and admiration for the revolution's accomplishments.

As foreign as it might seem to observers from the US, the top down controls imposed by the revolutionary regime appear to me as having been absolutely necessary. In the context of the Cold War and the US assaults, the Castro-led regime could not have achieved its remarkable advances without a unified front against powerful enemies. That unity depended in part on controls over economic activity and a strong national security apparatus. Playa Girón was but one example of what awaited them if they dropped their guard.

Further, having spent time in Mexico, where poverty and wealth stand side by side in stark, obscene contrast, and again in Guatemala where the oppressive presence of the military was felt everywhere, I could not deny that Cubans had built a society with far more equitable distribution of the resources and wealth of their country. The popular support for the revolution was undeniably widespread as well. Contrary to the mainstream narrative in the US, most people in the island nation recognized their plight was far less dire than it had been, and equally that their lives were far better than they might have been without the advent of the Castro-led regime.

Still, unanswered questions remain with me to this day. They are largely about whether the siege mentality I encountered in Cuba, and have since experienced in other revolutionary settings, are the price of admission for regimes pursuing radical transformations. When that question was taken head on during The Brigade's time in Cuba, some argued it was a transitional reality, at times linking it to Marx's description in *The Communist Manifesto* of the dictatorship of the proletariat. Revolutions, they argued, must go through a period of transition in which they battle the resistance of the old ways and the powerful established interests that are not about to relinquish their privileges and power. Only then, the argument goes, can those revolutionary societies evolve into a world where equality and harmony are a common state of affairs.

But the question of a transitional reality has become all the more pressing as the decades have passed, not only in Cuba but in other revolutions. Is the authoritarian tendency that seems to gain strength over time in these revolutions, and the suppression of political and social discourse and diversity that appears to accompany it, inherent in the revolutionary project, as critics would have us believe, or is this tendency a conjunctural aberration largely imposed by external opposition that may eventually be overcome, as proponents of revolutions would argue?

My other great frustration while in Cuba was my inability to dig deeper into the lives of everyday people. The whole brigade experience was one of orchestrated encounters crammed into an intense and brief time frame. I had little space for reflection or the revisiting of unresolved concerns. I came to realize that problems, like accomplishments, were far too complex to fully understand in such a constrained environment.

Some years later I would address both these questions by living nearly five years in the midst of the Nicaraguan Revolution. Rather than rely on a guided tour, this time I would immerse myself in the everyday lives of people living through a revolution. It is to that venture, and more specifically to the individuals I came to know, that the following essays now turn.

III. Nicaragua: A Time of Revolution

By the mid-1970s the Vietnam War had come to an end. The war had opened the eyes of many of my generation to the deceit and deception of a US government pursuing Cold War, imperial ambitions across the globe. The massive protests and opposition to the war at the end of the previous decade had raised the specter of a social revolution within the United States. While such a prospect soon subsided, it drew the attention of many progressive people to the potential of revolutions and liberation movements around the world as they sought to break free of an oppressive colonial history. Solidarity movements became a logical graduation for some from the anti-war and other efforts of the preceding decade. Solidarity with the Cuban Revolution, the anti-apartheid movement in South Africa, and Central American revolutionary movements, captured the imagination of many progressive people in the US

My journey through the Cuban Revolution during that time, while exhilarating, in some ways became the zenith of my avidity for revolutionary change as it led to a questioning of the truths and shibboleths of radical doctrine. The political fervor of the prior decade had begun to give way to doubts among many of us about what my generation's passions were achieving. While we still embraced a fundamental belief in the good that came from greater equality, and the commensurate evil that persisted with gross inequities in power and wealth, we had begun to question the wisdom of the revolutionary path to social change. In my case, that old demon of doubt that had led me away from religion in my childhood, and from any number of callings as a young man, was gnawing at my soul once more. This time it was eroding my enthusiasm for the more extreme dimensions of the radical agenda. It was time to reassess the path forward.

I followed my Cuban experience with a six-year hiatus during which I pursued an academic investigation of those same questions, culminating in a doctoral degree in Sociology from the University of California, Santa Cruz. Then, within days of graduation, I renewed my exploration of revolutions from an up close and personal perspective. This time I decided to take a deeper dive, moving to Nicaragua in 1983 for what would become a nearly five-year immersion in a nascent revolution. This time, I was going to work with and come to know everyday people who, I realized, were the true measure of what was possible on this radical path into the future.

The context in which I set out on this new adventure had changed significantly. The 1980s were marked by the advent of the Reagan Revolution. In particular, the neo-conservative revival of a hawkish Cold War foreign policy dominated the United States' international relations. Nowhere was the renewed hardline politics more evident than in Central America.

Throughout the 1980s, Central America was a place of hope and despair. A 1979 insurrection had toppled the Somoza dictatorship in Nicaragua and established a revolutionary regime in its place. That same year a military coup just to the north in El Salvador overthrew a reformist military government and launched a civil war between a mix of moderate and leftist rebel groups and a brutally repressive military regime. Still further north, a force led by a mix of Mayan and *ladino* factions challenged another military-dominated government.

While many observers in the region recognized all these uprisings as a response to a long history of military regimes backed by rapacious landed elites, the Reagan administration held to a different view. Appearing to have learned little from the tragedy that was the Vietnam War, the neoconservatives that made up Reagan's inner circle saw another case of a communist menace to be staunched mercilessly by military force. The only lesson they took away from Vietnam was that this time, rather than send US troops into another conflict, they flooded the region with military aid. They used national armies as proxies in Guatemala and El Salvador and created a paramilitary force, the *Contra*, to invade Nicaragua.

The result was a bloodbath perhaps only surpassed by the Spanish Conquest. In Guatemala, the military wiped out over 400 indigenous communities during the decade on the premise that impoverished peasants were sympathetic to the rebels and thus a barrier to eliminating the threat to the old order. I visited several Mayan villages during that period and was met by populations of children, old people, and widowed women. Every male within a certain age had been taken away, many later found in mass graves and others never to be seen again.

In Nicaragua, over 50,000 people were killed, mostly innocent peasants, the victims of the proxy war carried out by the US backed *Contras*. El Salvador saw some of the most severe effects of Reagan's undeclared "low intensity" war. In the decade of the 1980s, over 100,000 people were killed, again the vast majority from the rural poor.

I arrived in Nicaragua at the height of the Sandinista-led revolution. Like so many others, I shared a hope that the revolution held out the promise of a better future for that country's impoverished majority. As such it also offered a unique opportunity for me to understand both the potential, and the limits, of revolutionary change. It was a period that remains among the most formative and powerful of my life.

That the Nicaraguan Revolution has not lived up to the lofty, some would say naïve expectations of its supporters, is neither the fault of those supporters nor, in some ways, even of the government led by the Sandinista Front for National Liberation. At least in hindsight, it seems somewhat predictable that the Nicaraguan Revolution would eventually falter in the face of the unrelenting pressures of the United States government.

To be clear, the Nicaraguan Revolution achieved significant advances, particularly for the rural poor. Further, the current Sandinista government, defeated electorally in 1990 and then reelected several times since, has implemented policies that benefit that same rural poor, including commitments to education, health care, and rural economic development. But the recent form of that revolutionary movement has become more ritual than substance. Over the past three decades an ever-narrower subgroup of what was once a dynamic and broad-based movement has increasingly adopted measures to maintain their hold on power at the expense of broadening or deepening the social transformations of the 1980s. Again, in hindsight, to have expected an alternative outcome given the unshaken commitment to quash any progressive social change by the behemoth that is the United States, may have been folly. It suggests such ventures in the future may require fundamental *a priori* (or at least parallel), changes at the heart of the problem, rather than beginning at its periphery.

But for me, the magic, and the legacy of that first decade of the revolution was to be found in the lives of everyday Nicaraguans, as well as those who came in solidarity from other places, rather than the government or party's promises. The following stories recall people I came to know and the lessons I learned from them about the prospects for, and challenges to, sweeping social change.

7. Gladys and Noel: A Love Story

Early one Saturday I drove from Managua through the regional capital of Matagalpa and up over a nearby mountain pass. The mountainsides were draped in the low-hanging mist of a semitropical rainforest, the dense green foliage dripping with heavy morning dew. Once out the other side, the terrain gave way to valleys and gently rising hills. The valley floor was carpeted in tall grasses of greens and yellows, framed by soft knolls crowned with large, solitary trees. It was a vision ever so reminiscent of the rolling hills and massive live oaks of the Napa Valley of my childhood.

My partner at the time, Laura, had made the acquaintance of a coffee farmer near El Tuma, east of Matagalpa, as part of her doctoral research on the ambitious Nicaraguan agrarian reform. We were to spend the weekend with Gladys and her husband, Noel, as Laura gathered data on the continued viability of coffee production under the Sandinista regime. This was, for me, an opportunity to get to know Nicaraguans living through the sweeping changes of a revolution barely five years in the making.

After thirty minutes traversing the lone dirt track along the valley floor, we began to climb again into lush and verdant forest. We drove through beautiful stands of what appeared to be cedars, others perhaps teak and massive baobabs, and still others totally foreign to me, covered in vines and bright flowers of soft pink, bright yellow, and fiery red. Beneath the forest canopy the floor was planted in six- to ten-foot coffee trees. It was the end of the harvest, so the limbs were no longer laden with clusters of bright red coffee cherries.

We arrived at the farm center, where a two-story, rustic wooden house, several outbuildings, and a row of mostly empty workers' quarters awaited us. After hugs and handshakes with Gladys and Noel, we settled into a lunch of rice, beans, tortillas, and stewed chicken. We dined under an open-sided corrugated tin roof over a dirt-floored patio, surrounded by a dark and thickly woven mass of jungle. We began with an extended conversation about the health and well-being of family members of all present, the requisite initiation of any Nicaraguan gathering. Then Gladys, acknowledging the purpose of our visit, began describing the farm and its history.

The family owned several coffee farms, with Gladys and Noel managing two. The family coffee business was started by Gladys's grandfather, John Bolt, an Englishman who came to Nicaragua in the early twentieth century to prospect for gold. He soon shifted to coffee, as had numerous other nineteenth- and early twentieth-century European adventurers. The Nicaraguan coffee industry developed much as had the Salvadoran and Guatemalan industries just to the north, with larger-scale plantations displacing small-holding indigenous farmers through both legal and illegal means. The Bolts were not among the largest of coffee growers, whose estates were mostly in the nearby Granada region, fifty miles to the southwest. But they were still considered part of the coffee oligarchy, a label synonymous with concentrated wealth nested in severe rural poverty.

John Bolt married a Nicaraguan woman and they had several children, Gladys's father, Guillermo, among them. Gladys was one of several children who grew up in the relative affluence of the coffee oligarchs. As was tradition among the Nicaraguan elite, Gladys went to the United States in her teens to be educated and see the world. It was perhaps a reflection of the times and the cultural changes emerging in the 1960s that the Bolt children began to diverge from the oligarchy's traditions and values, a generational break that would mark them years later as traitors to their class.

Gladys suspected that her father sending her north was not entirely motivated by his desire to see her educated. She had grown enamored with a young man by the name of Noel Rivera, and her father seemed eager to stifle their budding romance. But Noel followed her to the US, where he worked a warehouse night shift while courting Gladys. Not long after, they returned to Nicaragua, an unlikely union of a working-class young man and the daughter of an oligarch. They married and began to pursue the family tradition of coffee and cattle production.

We soon drifted away from questions of acreage, yields, wages, and other details important to my companion's research. We found ourselves in an amusing exchange about where each of us was in the period after Gladys and Noel first met. Their descriptions of wandering through San Francisco's Haight-Ashbury and witnessing the 1967 Summer of Love had all of us laughing—at times trying to translate colloquialisms of the time or lyrics of songs. I confess I was and remain incapable of explaining the meaning of Donovan's "Mellow Yellow." It was a wonderful afternoon of hilarious cross-cultural confusion.

On their return to Nicaragua, near the end of the 1960s, Gladys and Noel began to create a different culture around their coffee farm. They routinely brought health workers to run clinics for the workers and their families. Historically, health care was largely inaccessible to the rural poor. They brought teachers to provide what minimal education the children could pursue during the several months-long harvest season, again an opportunity not otherwise available to those same workers. They tried as they could to make inroads into the paternalistic owner-worker relationship that underpinned the feudal world of migrant labor, the foundation of the accumulated wealth and commensurate poverty found in the coffee sector throughout Latin America.

Not surprisingly, Gladys and Noel became involved in the incipient efforts to overthrow the Somoza dynasty, a single-family rule that ran back over fifty years. They were not part of the Sandinista Front for National Liberation, as the revolutionary movement was known. But neither were they far from the ideals of the growing opposition to the Somoza dictatorship. On several occasions Noel had opened the farm as a refuge for young people fleeing the Nicaraguan National Guard. The "Guardia" was a police force that did Somoza's bidding and was increasingly rounding up university students and others, torturing and in some cases "disappearing" them under suspicion of being sympathetic to the Sandinistas.

Gladys was involved in organizing farmers in the region to resist efforts to steal land or businesses or to impose harsh taxes and other controls on agricultural producers not part of the dictator's loyal inner circle. The growing opposition throughout Nicaragua turned into insurrection, culminating in the overthrow of Somoza in 1979. With the subsequent launching of the Nicaraguan revolutionary government, Gladys and Noel continued to focus their lives on farming. While many of the coffee oligarchy fled the country and had their plantations nationalized, Gladys and Noel became part of a small but successful private farming sector embraced, or at least tolerated, by the socialist government.

As the sun set low in the treetops, Gladys and Noel excused themselves—Gladys to join the cook in the cookhouse to prepare a large meal in celebration of the end of the harvest, while Noel headed back into town. The feast would be for the workers who had remained an extra day or two on the plantation and those who lived in nearby villages. Noel would return in a few hours with a band to liven up the festivities.

Darkness falls in the tropical forest like a blackout curtain drawn slowly across a sunlit window. In a matter of minutes, the fading light through the bush gave way to an impenetrable wall of night just beyond our small circle around a fire pit. The temperature dropped just as quickly. A generator started, and electric lights, strung around the nearby open dining area, flickered to life. Soon the workers and their children began to appear at the door to the cookhouse. Heaping plates of food—tamales, plantain, rice and beans, tortillas, and grilled strips of beef—were being passed along to families gathering at the tables. There was much laughter and chatter, an atmosphere of ease that belied the stark class differences that undeniably still existed between the workers and owners, not to mention their American guests.

As we were eating, Noel arrived from town, the cab and back of his aging and rusted truck packed with musicians and instruments. Soon the band was set up, the tables cleared, plates gathered back in the kitchen, and the music began. Noel and Gladys moved to the patio and began gliding through a scattering of dancers, holding each other at arm's length while gazing into each other's eyes with dreamlike smiles. They swayed to the rhythm of Cumbia, Colombian music popular throughout the Americas. They floated beautifully together in that Latin way, reminding me of what millennia of repressed sensuality had taken from those of us whose emotional centers remained rooted in the painfully self-conscious Anglo-Saxon world. I remember thinking that they looked as deeply in love as I imagined they were when they met decades back.

The next morning after breakfast, Noel took us up into the rainforest outside the farm compound. Several children, both theirs and those of the workers, came along. We walked up a path, the coffee plants and shade trees to one side. The undergrowth of uncleared jungle on the other side was a riot of broad-leaf plants, tangled flowering vines, and huge ferns beneath a dense and heavy overstory. The light filtered through in deep greens and dark shadows, the air humid, thick, and warm. It was an immersion into an otherworldly array of colors, smells, and sensations of a semitropical rainforest. I drifted as much as strolled along the path away from the compound and into the enveloping jungle.

We came to a steep hillside, and Noel and the children scrambled upwards twenty or thirty feet to a soft, moss-covered shelf, with Laura and me following on unsteady legs. Noel handed me a *liana*, an inch-thick, ropelike vine that hung from high in the treetops. Each of the kids took one as well and without hesitation threw themselves out over the chasm dropping away beneath us. I gave it a tentative try, thinking the vine could not possibly hold, expecting to plummet down the hillside. But hold it did, and I found myself whooping and grinning as I swung farther and farther over the jungle below. With several more ambitious leaps from the shelf, I felt like Tarzan flying through the forest canopy. The kids and Noel just grinned with placid gazes, perhaps pondering: *You'd think this American had never been in a jungle before.*

After lunch we shared hugs all around and set out on the long dirt road back to Matagalpa and then down the mountainside to the Pacific coastal plain and our house in the hills south of Managua. It had been a magical weekend with our most wonderful hosts that remains vividly etched in my memory to this day. I looked forward to the next visit both to spend more time talking and laughing with Gladys and Noel and to again lose myself in that idyllic tropical forest in the far reaches of the wild and remote mountains of central Nicaragua.

We returned to our daily routines in Managua, and as the weeks went by, I thought less and less about that special weekend. Work and getting through the daily grind of life in a city of over a million people in the throes of revolutionary change and in an undeclared war with the United States government was all-consuming. One morning I opened the daily newspaper as I sat down for a cup of coffee and skimmed the front page. The headlines screamed of the threats of North American imperialism and the injustices of the Reagan administration's blockade of the Nicaraguan economy. I was somewhat numb to the media expressions of outrage, justified as they were, as I drifted down the page. I came to the near-daily column documenting the deaths resulting from the incursions across the border from Honduras by the US-backed Contras. The Contras were paramilitary, right-wing rebel groups funded by the US government and trained by the CIA, made up mostly of ex-Somoza National Guardsmen. The Contra groups moved into isolated parts of Nicaragua and attacked military outposts and infrastructure targets to undermine the Sandinista presence in remote regions of the country and to disrupt the already teetering economy.

I scanned the names as one might a passenger list of a plane crash in some distant place, not expecting to recognize anyone. But there near the top of the list was Noel Rivera Morraz, ambushed in the Matagalpa province several days prior. I did not recognize the last name. Most Nicaraguans have several last names reflecting their family lineage. Noel was also a relatively common first name, just as Rivera was a common surname. Still, I wondered. The other names were of rural villagers and local militia members, the most common victims of the war. The landed elite were not the targets of guerilla insurgency. I dismissed the possibility that this was our Noel and set the paper aside.

I had plans to meet with Laura and Carlos, a Nicaraguan colleague of hers, at a local café for lunch. As I walked into the small restaurant they looked up from their booth, and my heart dropped. It was on both their faces. It was our Noel—Gladys and her children's Noel—who was on that list. I slid into the booth and stared at them. In a near whisper I asked, "What happened?" Carlos began to speak, as Laura was clearly in no shape to reply.

Noel was driving out to the farm from a shopping trip to town on that dirt road along the valley floor we had traveled just weeks before. As he came around a bend, a Contra force of roughly twenty-five men blocked the road and surrounded him, dragging him from his pickup. They tied him to a nearby tree, then proceeded to torture him, according to what Carlos had learned from friends in Matagalpa. They used bayonets to cut him repeatedly. Then they took turns kicking and beating him until his ribs were broken and his chest crushed, leaving him to die at the side of the road.

When he did not arrive at the farm, his son-in-law went searching, finding him the next morning. One day later the same band attacked a nearby village, taking eight men who were deemed Sandinista sympathizers and cutting their throats while their families and the rest of the villagers were forced to watch. They decapitated two of the victims and left their heads on fence posts along the road. They went on to burn down Gladys and Noel's farm.

I finally found my voice, barely. "And Gladys?"

"She is with family in Matagalpa," Carlos said. "She is devastated."

He went on to explain that killing Noel was part of a recent escalation in Contra and US strategy to undermine the rural economy and thereby increase shortages and hardships to weaken popular support. It was meant to drive farmers and others from the rural areas that produced much of what Nicaraguans ate and what the government relied upon for foreign currency to buy everything from fuel to medicines. And the strategy was working. Many of the larger-scale farmers refused to travel out to their farms. Villagers and small-scale farmers either migrated into Managua or banded into armed encampments for protection, rarely venturing out into their fields.

But the tragedy did not stop Gladys. Within months she was back organizing farmers and speaking to visiting "fact-finding" delegations from the United States and Europe. She spoke to whoever would listen. She talked of what it meant to not be a member of the Sandinista Party but still committed to building a better Nicaragua, just like her husband. She went to Washington to testify before the US Congress in an attempt to make Americans understand that contrary to the official US version, the Contras were not a force of "freedom fighters" engaged in liberating their country. They were mostly aggrieved members of the former dictator's "Guardia," murdering innocent civilians as they had before their overthrow in the hopes of reestablishing their former rule. Noel and thousands of other noncombatants were the real targets of the war.

Her testimony fell on deaf ears in the Reagan White House and among the Republican Party in Congress. While some in the Democratic Party campaigned mightily against further funding of the Contras, the Reagan administration found legal and illegal means, including the infamous Iran-Contra affair, to continue financing the bloodshed. Gladys never returned to the farm and she forbade her children from ever returning as well.

In 1985, a year after Noel's death, American journalist Ron Ridenour was part of a visiting delegation that met with a group of Nicaraguan farmers. Gladys was among them. In his book, *Yankee Sandinistas*, Ridenour described a dinner in which he was seated beside Gladys. "After food was served a mariachi band struck up gay dance music. Tears dropped gently onto Gladys's plate as she watched. She whispered to me, 'I miss Noel so much. I haven't danced since they killed my lovely husband.'"

I never saw Gladys again, but I have often recalled that loving couple, their beautiful children, and the time we shared in that magical place. In the nearly four decades since, I have pondered many times the tragedy that war visited upon them. The Contra war, President Reagan told us, was fought in defense of freedom, democracy, and the American way of life. It was waged against godless communists, just as the Vietnam War and so many others before had been. But such abstractions dehumanized and obscured a deeper reality. The majority of victims were not combatants. They were civilians, people living their lives, raising their families, and pursuing their dreams. The superpower contests and ideology-driven trope that defined US foreign policy were worlds away.

Whatever the justification for the endless conflicts that rage on to this day, the true cost of those ignoble adventures has been the snuffing out of the lives of innocents on an incomprehensible scale. I cannot believe there is any cause worthy of such a price. For me the choice was made back in that moment now long past. I will forever be on the side of the Gladyses and Noels and celebrate the love stories of all the other nameless people in far-off places who deserve nothing less than to live out their lives in peace in a manner of their own choosing.

8. El Poeta

Not long after I arrived in Nicaragua, I began working on a project to reduce the extremely high rate of pesticide-related illnesses in the coastal province of León. The project team was made up of a doctor, Feliciano Pacheco, a nurse, Consuelo "Conie" Rodriquez, and a labor inspector, Enrique Fonseca, known as "El Poeta." We spent endless days driving through stifling, hot and dusty fields, and along barely passable backroads, to reach large cotton plantations. We would conduct medical exams, safety inspections, and training sessions for workers handling or exposed to agricultural chemicals. Over several years we repeatedly visited nearly every cotton plantation in the region, and in the process our little team became not only colleagues but friends.

Most days began at sunrise, and we often arrived at the farm centers unannounced. We would conduct our inspections of the workplaces and visit the families living adjacent to the cotton fields in one-room huts, looking for indications of pesticide-related illness. In an epidemiological study, a Nicaraguan university team found that roughly ten thousand workers in the region had been poisoned at least once in the previous season. The health problem was as pervasive as it was serious.

When the workers came in from the fields to the cookhouse for lunch, we were able to run a series of medical tests and brief education sessions. After the workers returned to the fields and before we packed up to leave, the farm manager would usually offer us lunch, which amounted to whatever had been prepared for the workers. The regular meal at nearly every farm was a plate of white rice, a slice of boiled plantain, and a small tortilla. Bulk over variety was the standard fare. For the special guests a bottle of soda was added, usually a ghastly local beverage called Rojita, or an even worse milky-white soft drink called Chele, the latter becoming a nickname for the pale-skinned foreigners like myself. We got so we looked forward to visiting one farm, El Toro Blanco (the White Bull), because the cook sometimes sprinkled parsley into the rice, making it distinctly more flavorful than the generic offering at the other plantations. I became a connoisseur of worker cuisine over those endless days and months in the almost unbearably hot lowlands of northwestern Nicaragua.

Enrique would regale us over the interminable hours waiting under a shade tree for workers to arrive, or during the long road trips out to the farms. Sometimes he would recite his poetry and other times he would tell tales that wandered from important events in recent Nicaraguan history to fantastical descriptions of moments hundreds of years in the past. Every story Enrique told was in first-person.

At first I had a hard time following, since my Spanish was not up to Enrique's rapid and slang-laden oration. As I became more accustomed to his habit of dropping consonants and vowels at the beginning and end of many words, I began to glean the gist of his tales and as I did, I would often stop him and say, "Wait, this happened when?" and he would patiently answer with something like, "When the Spaniards began taking our lands." I would look to Dr. Pacheco and he would smile and nod as if to say, "That's right. Sometime in the seventeenth century."

I would then turn to Conie and she would smile and nod, an eyebrow raised, her head cocked slightly to one side with a look implying "Is there something you are not understanding?"

Many days I returned home late in the evening, totally exhausted, perhaps as much from the torturous process of following Enrique's stories as they leaped backward and forward across centuries as from bouncing through hot and dusty cotton fields.

Gradually I began to better understand Enrique. I came to realize he was sharing a centuries-old tradition: the passing on of an indigenous collective memory through the retelling of a community-shared oral history. Enrique was from Sutiaba, an indigenous community on the outskirts of the city of León that claimed its ancestry as indigenous people of the same name rather than from the Spanish conquerors. Feliciano was also a Sutiaba. I began to learn of the important role his community had played in the resistance to the Spaniards, then to the ladino elites of León, and finally against the Somoza dictatorship. Little by little I grasped the critical role the Sutiabas played throughout Nicaraguan history in fighting the otherwise largely successful efforts to wipe out indigenous traditions. The Sutiabas became widely known for their strong and at times violent resistance and, in the post-World War II era, in the organizing of a significant element of what would become the Sandinista revolutionary movement. Enrique appeared, at least by his telling, to have been in the middle of it all.

Throughout much of the twentieth century the large landowners of the region sought to put an end to communally owned indigenous lands, annexing the community of Sutiaba and all its holdings to the nearby City of León in 1902. It was cynically claimed to be a "civilizing" measure necessary to turn primitive indigenous peoples into "proper" Nicaraguans, which primarily took the form of making them individual private property owners. The strategy had worked well in the coffee-growing regions throughout Central America over the preceding half-century, as various measures involving land titling, bank lending, taxation, and outright theft led to indigenous private properties increasingly becoming large plantations owned by the ladino elites.

By the end of World War II, the ladino assault on indigenous lands and cultures appeared to have been largely successful. In 1953 anthropologist Richard Adams observed that the Sutiabas no longer used an indigenous language, wore only ladino clothing, and lacked other indigenous cultural indicators. He concluded that the claim to being indigenous no longer had any objective basis.

Yet just one year after Adams's famous *Cultural Survey of Central America*, the Sutiabas revived a long moribund political organization called *La Comunidad Indígena*. They began resisting the continued incursions and appropriations of their communal lands. Enrique described how delegations of elected representatives of the *Comunidad Indígena* would confront the officials from León in an array of public venues. The Sutiabas recognized their own political representatives over those of the ladino local government and pursued claims in the name of the indigenous community. On other occasions, groups from Sutiaba would block roads to and from the city that passed through what had been indigenous lands. This was part of a broader strategy to slow or halt the eradication of their lives as a people.

The confrontations at times became violent, and the Sutiabas came to be known as aggressive in the defense of their ancestral lands. Enrique would describe in detail how secret meetings occurred in village houses at night and how messages would be passed before launching a daylight action. Some stories, or poems, would describe the use of the *atabales* and the *son*, drums that would signal a call to gather or to take action. On other occasions he would describe the role of festival dances like the Giant Pepe and Dance of the Bull in maintaining a memory of battles waged centuries earlier. From the point of that political organizational revival forward, many of the cultural artifacts scholars deemed essential to being indigenous were increasingly on display.

On one trip to a cotton farm called Punta Ñata, at the far northern tip of the Nicaraguan coastal plain, our arrival was delayed by several hours while the road was choked with soldiers filing back toward the south. When we finally arrived, the farm center was nearly deserted. We were told that in the early morning the Contras had attacked from the sea, thus explaining the heavy military movement we passed on the way. The assailants used fast boats, called *piranhas*, built in Argentina and provided by the CIA. The piranha had a mortar mounted in the front allowing the attackers to approach silently right up to the cliffs along the shore that bordered the farm, fire their rockets, and then make a high-speed escape to their base across the Gulf of Fonseca in Honduras.

After talking briefly with the farm manager, Enrique took me out into the adjacent cotton field. About fifty yards from the compound where we had been scheduled to conduct the health clinic, we found a small crater in the ground where the rocket had exploded. Enrique pointed out how the crater was relatively shallow, perhaps only a foot deep, but the surrounding vegetation was completely shredded for a radius of thirty yards or more.

"It was an antipersonnel rocket filled with shrapnel," he said, "meant to maim and kill the people who came to our clinic this morning." He glanced over at me and with a wan smile added, "And us."

As we abandoned our day's efforts and returned to town, Enrique railed on. The Contras, he said, were like the Spaniards. They would not confront brave warriors in combat, but instead would sneak up under the cover of darkness that protected them from the defenses of simple peasants.

"They did the same thing to us when they captured our great leader, the *cacique* Adiac. They seized him while we slept, then took him to the great Tamarindon near the village center. When we heard the soldiers moving through the village we rushed into the streets, but there were too many and they had weapons we could not match. They hanged Adiac from that tree. There was nothing we could do to stop them. This is what the Contras learned from the Spaniards."

"Wait." I tried again in what was undoubtedly by now a familiar plaintive refrain, "The Spaniards? When was this? You were there?" Conie and Feliciano chuckled and shook their heads once again. I later learned that the Spaniards hanged Adiac in 1610. The tamarind tree where it supposedly happened, known as the Tamarindon, still stands in the village square of Sutiaba.

At that point in our many trips to the countryside, I knew better than to question Enrique about the impossibility of his eyewitness accounts that nonindigenous historians still debate as having even occurred. Many questioned whether Adiac ever existed, but I had long given up on trying to discern the veracity of Enrique's stories against conventional Western historiography. Instead, I just listened in wonder and tried to tolerate the headache I invariably got laboring to follow this rich, first-person narration.

On another occasion, while waiting for the workers to arrive at a farm center, Enrique and Feliciano began talking about the Sandinistas and their erstwhile attempts to build a revolutionary movement. They laughed about the naïve but impassioned young students who came to Sutiaba from the nearby university in León, hoping to convince the community to revolt against Somoza.

"They were spouting slogans from Marx and Lenin, telling us we should throw off the shackles of our oppressors and their imperialist masters in the United States. As if we had not already been fighting for our land and our people for hundreds of years. We quickly decided we needed to teach these students how to get organized before they all got themselves killed, and many of them did anyway."

I leaned over and whispered to Conie, "They are referring to the period of militancy from the mid-1950s. At least I know they were young men in their twenties and thus could actually have been there. For once this makes sense."

Conie gave me that same tired, but patient look and said something like, "That does not make the story any more or less true than all the others."

I felt another headache coming on.

But I soon realized I was being given a privileged insight into how an indigenous struggle to protect an ancient culture had coalesced with a twentieth-century insurrection-in-the-making, and once again, Enrique seemed to be right in the middle of it. At the time I could not quite figure out what was true and what was fantasy. More than once I wondered if after I left each evening, they had a good laugh and planned the next great yarn they would spin for the gullible American.

After nearly five years traversing the cotton fields around León, I returned to the United States. On a couple of occasions, I received and returned well-wishes with Feliciano and Enrique. I never connected with Conie again. Three decades later I learned that Enrique had become something of a cult figure among scholars from around the world. His propensity for telling stories in vivid detail turned out to be a remarkable font of historical record. Academic articles and books had been published relying upon, and in many ways validating, Enrique's rich accounts of an indigenous history and culture otherwise largely undocumented or discredited by ladino scholars. But Enrique and a few others persisted in telling their stories, maintaining a legend despite Western traditions.

Enrique's steadfast commitment to telling and documenting Sutiaba history helps explain the relatively vibrant cultural survival Sutiaba enjoys today. A decade before Enrique began to receive such notoriety, I had been treated to the stories of an oracle from another world into which I unknowingly was given a privileged glimpse. Enrique died in 2015 at the age of eighty-five.

9. I Can't Just Leave

Throughout the nearly five years I lived in Nicaragua, I attended monthly meetings of the Committee of United States Citizens Living in Nicaragua (CUSCLIN). We met in a church at the south end of Managua. It was an unlikely gathering of nuns and lay people, journalists, the American spouses of several Nicaraguans, a few people like me working in humanitarian organizations, and others with varying reasons for being long-term residents. These meetings would take several hours and mostly involved sharing updates on projects in the country, analyses of US or Nicaraguan government actions, and planning the infrequent protests in front of the US embassy. The CUSCLIN meetings were also a common place for newly arrived people from the US to make contacts and get help navigating the sometimes Kafkaesque bureaucratic hurdles encountered by well-meaning but often clueless Americans seeking to become a part of the Nicaraguan Revolution.

At one such meeting a young man sat next to me as the meeting began. With a slight build, thick, round glasses, and a smile full of teeth, he reached over to shake hands and said, "Hi, I'm Ben."

He looked to still be in his late teens but was probably in his mid-twenties. He could not have weighed more than a buck twenty-five and seemed to be constantly amused as his gaze drifted over the gathered. He explained he had recently arrived and "wanted to check out what was going on."

Once started, the meeting rambled through its regular details. It began with a discussion of an Embassy demonstration that would occur in two weeks. Everyone was cautioned to be respectful and look out for provocateurs. An elderly midwestern pastor warned us there would be no flag burning or throwing red paint on the embassy walls. He was a veteran of the US military and reminded us that the American public was watching to see what US citizens in Nicaragua were about. Another chimed in that we would only be taken seriously if we appeared to be what we were, a cross-section of American society and not a bunch of crazed leftists, of which there were several as well.

A number of other announcements followed—a US journalist was looking for interviews with people working in the countryside; an update on a project on the Atlantic Coast among the Miskitu indigenous communities; a reminder that volunteering for the cotton and coffee harvests would be a great place to show solidarity with the rural poor; and on and on. As the meeting began to break up, Ben turned to me and said, "Do you do anything more than have meetings?"

Not sure what he meant, I responded with a furrowed brow, "Like what?"

"You know, parties. Don't you guys have fun?"

I shook my head and tried to hide my incredulity, "This is a pretty serious bunch. Not sure I have heard of any parties."

With his unflagging grin he just gazed back as if waiting for me to say, "Just kidding."

I wasn't. Fortunately for both of us, someone stopped by and asked me if I had a minute to discuss something, and I quickly took my leave.

At the next meeting Ben wandered in, spotted me, and came over to sit next to me. It appeared he had befriended me, an honor I had not yet quite warmed to. After a nod of greeting, we sat through another long meeting. At the end he turned and asked, "How did you get a visa to stay here? I keep being told it's not possible, and yet here you all are. What am I missing?"

I explained the government made it difficult, especially for US citizens, to stay in-country. There was a justifiable paranoia about what motivated the hundreds of foreigners that came through each month. There were undoubtedly agents from various intelligence services moving around Managua with something less than solidarity in their hearts. I told him that most of us had some sort of sponsor. I had worked as a volunteer for the Ministry of Labor when I arrived and then started a health project with funding and sponsorship from a group of humanitarian organizations.

He seemed bewildered. Like so many before him, he assumed good intentions were all that mattered, and he expected the Nicaraguans to welcome people of goodwill with open arms. He was learning, as many of us had, that the revolution was a complicated affair and not for the easily deterred. Unfortunately, the immigration service and visa process had foiled many well-meaning visitors, sending some back to the states complaining of ungrateful Nicaraguans and a xenophobic Sandinista party.

Ben was back the next month and explained he had found a volunteer position with the Nicaraguan Institute of Energy. With his degree in mechanical engineering, he discovered he had some useful skills in the energy sector. But he also found the agency to be a difficult place to work. People showed up at their offices irregularly, missed meetings frequently, and most importantly, the managers who promised to get his visa approved failed to deliver.

I had similar experiences. Most of the lower-to-midlevel managers were Sandinista militants with limited or no previous managerial skills, and in many cases with very little training in whatever agency mission they found themselves. Many of the educated and trained middle class and elites that traditionally occupied these posts had fled the country during the insurrection or soon after the Sandinistas came to power. So people were making it up on the fly. It was a frustrating and challenging situation for volunteers from the industrialized world accustomed to a rules-driven, albeit also inefficient, bureaucracy.

Ben eventually succeeded in getting his visa and continued to work in an increasingly chaotic government sector. I had to give him credit for persevering. But Ben not only stuck with it, he soon began to thrive. He had become somewhat of a personality in a little neighborhood near the shore of Lake Managua where he lived. He had years earlier taken up a hobby as a circus clown and had apparently been trained quite well. He performed at events in his neighborhood, riding through the streets on a unicycle while juggling various objects, with complete clown attire and face paint. He often performed as part of a campaign, anything from neighborhood cleanup to getting children out for a vaccination clinic.

He also went to the countryside with his colleagues from the government ministry to volunteer in the cotton harvest. This had become an important annual undertaking that gave young urban Nicaraguans in particular a shared experience of being part of the effort to support the revolution. Ben was becoming accepted, and increasingly invested, in the Nicaraguan Revolution. I suspect he was also finding the occasional party along the way.

My attendance at the CUSCLIN meetings grew infrequent, as I worked much of my time in the northwestern region of León. I did not get into Managua as often as I had initially. I lost touch with Ben and did not see him for more than a year. But when I did make it to a meeting I often heard impressive accounts of Ben's work. He had moved to a poor rural village in the northcentral part of the country, a small community called El Cua. Nicaragua had the lowest rate of electrified households in the region. Ben began working with a team from the Energy Institute that included both Nicaraguans and other international volunteers, constructing a very small-scale hydroelectric plant on a nearby stream. With the construction of a micro dam and installation of a small water-driven generator, they were developing an innovative and appropriate technology for these poor rural areas, bringing light to a community that had never had electricity. It was an inspiring undertaking. Ben had found a place in the Nicaraguan Revolution, and he was making the most of it.

Then Ben showed up at one of those rare CUSCLIN meetings that I was able to attend. I found myself grinning back in response to his toothy smile—I was genuinely happy to see him. We did not have a chance to talk, as the meeting was already underway. I had to run off after the meeting. But before I left, Ben pulled me aside and asked if I had time to talk. We arranged to meet that next weekend at my one-room cottage up on a hilltop above Managua.

When Ben arrived, we pulled two rocking chairs—iconic products from the crafts market in Masaya—out onto the grassy knoll overlooking Lake Managua and the city. We each opened a bottle of the local beer, Victoria, and for a few minutes just sat quietly and took in the view. Ben had changed. He had a scraggly beard that looked a bit like a post-adolescent's first attempt at facial hair, further accentuating his youthful appearance. But looking closer, I saw that he had aged. His gaze was more serious, and where he had always seemed brimming with enthusiasm, he now had a fatigued and pensive edge.

I began by complimenting him on what I knew of his remarkable work. But Ben cut me off and got directly to the point of his visit. "There have been several Contra radio broadcasts warning off foreigners from working in the region around our project. A couple have actually referred to me by name."

I had heard of the occasional broadcast leveling threats at the international community. I had not heard of anyone being called out by name. Several years earlier, another American volunteer—working near Sebaco in the central region of the country—shared with me after a Contra attack, less than five miles from the mechanics school he was running, that he doubted the Contras would target an American. But he also acknowledged he was wary. Most of us shared both his sense of relative security and his caution.

But the Contras had been escalating their forays into Nicaragua and had become more ruthless in their attacks on civilians and nonmilitary targets, so I knew the threat was not to be minimized.

"What," I asked, "were the local authorities telling you?"

Ben said they were taking the threats seriously, and at least one local official had questioned whether it might be prudent for Ben to leave.

"So, what are you thinking?" I asked.

"I can't just leave," he responded. "It feels like I'm abandoning people who are looking to me for help."

We both knew that there was an underlying tension in the internationalist community as to how serious we were about staying through the hard times likely yet to come. The usually unspoken truth was we all had safe havens to retreat to in our home country.

"Maybe you should give that some thought," I offered. While I recognized his passion for the moment, I found myself reflecting on all of our experiences over the preceding years. I had begun to realize that what we had imagined as both a radical and rapid process of change was going to be a long journey, the outcome of which was increasingly unclear. Nearing forty years of age, I was wondering if I was perhaps losing my youthful fervor.

Ben shook his head and sighed. It occurred to me he might have had the same impression.

"I can't just leave," he repeated, as if this was the central dilemma to which he always returned.

I tried again. "Maybe stay here in Managua for a month or two and see if the threats subside. I know the Sandinista army is moving through that region trying to intercept the invading bands. Even if you had to wait six months, you still could go back and pick up where you left off."

I could not tell if he was listening. He was not yet persuaded by my appeal, that much seemed clear. We sat quietly for another lengthy pause.

Finally, he said, "I just don't know. But I appreciate your hearing me out."

I responded, "Why don't you think about it a bit more. Give me a call and we can discuss it further. There can't be any big rush."

We finished our beer and he rose to leave. I tried one more time. "It's a long slog, this business of social change. A pause is not defeat. It's just a pause."

I got a tired smile in response, and Ben said he would think about it.

Weeks turned into months, and I did not hear back from Ben. I was totally engrossed in my own project, traveling around the cotton fields near León and working long hours away from home back in Managua. One evening upon returning to my little cottage I turned on my black-and-white TV with its twelve inch screen, to the state-run news broadcast, one of only two channels in the country. Before I could sit down and catch the latest stories I was hit with a picture of Ben, what appeared to be a passport photo, and a gut-wrenching opening storyline"

"Officials in Matagalpa have confirmed that American engineer Benjamin Linder was killed in a Contra ambush yesterday near the village of El Cua." I was frozen in place, my stomach in a knot. I didn't even know he had returned to his project. I sank into my chair and watched as the few facts available were repeated several times, then the news moved on to another story. I remember sitting there, alone, feeling profoundly tired. I turned off the news and sat in silence. I put my face in my hands and wiped away tears.

I learned more details in the ensuing days. Ben had returned to his hydroelectric project not long after our visit. There were conflicting stories about the ambush, but it appeared that a band of Contras had lain in wait at the dam site. When Ben and two Nicaraguan colleagues went down to the riverside to begin work, a grenade was thrown amongst them. All three were wounded in the explosion and lay incapacitated. The Contras had then shot each of them in the head at point-blank range. They were summarily executed.

There was widespread outrage in both national and international circles. This was the first instance in which an American had been purposely targeted and killed. In our little circle of Americans living in Nicaragua, there was only heartbreak. A funeral was held with President Daniel Ortega serving as a pallbearer. Ben's parents and siblings came from the States and walked in the procession. A second wake was held in a small church for family and friends in Ben's former neighborhood by the lake. I sat in the pew directly behind his parents. His mom seemed lost, bewildered, and leaned motionless against her husband's shoulder. Ben's father was stoic, appearing hollowed out. It was heart-rending.

In the following months, Ben's parents testified before a congressional hearing in Washington DC. They were brutally chastised by Republican members, the basic message being that Americans who put themselves in harm's way have no reason to expect sympathy. The politicians ignored the question of how a paramilitary group trained, funded, and directed by the US Central Intelligence Agency could first warn off an American by name, clearly target him in ambush, execute him, and then act as if the US government was not complicit in his murder.

For those of us living and working in Nicaragua, there was some soul-searching. I do not know of anyone who left because of the escalating Contra violence. But I also don't know of anyone who did not feel Ben's loss personally. He was one of the youngest of our US citizens' group. He had endured all the difficulties most of the rest of us had and succeeded in making a real difference in the lives of the rural poor. He had grown before our eyes. His death was for many of us an end to any illusions we might have harbored about what living and working in the Nicaraguan Revolution meant. I doubt any of us went to work again out in the countryside without recognizing that we could become a target.

Ben's murder also spoke to what it meant to be an American to the political forces back home. Clearly we were becoming a problem for the Reagan Administration's efforts to construct a dehumanized narrative about the revolution. We could only expect increasing pressure to leave. That most everyone I knew did not was a small source of pride. But it was countered by the sadness that stayed with all of us. Both the pride and the sadness return, I am sure, to all who lived through those years in Nicaragua, as it does to me to this day.

10. Free Diving With Guido

I began free diving in Nicaragua in 1984. An extreme sport, free diving was my escape from the intense living and working conditions of that time and place, and it became a passion that has remained with me ever since.

Through friends I was introduced to a young Italian named Guido who taught scuba diving, and I began taking lessons on weekends. But I soon learned that this affable young man's real passion was free diving. According to rumor, Guido had been an understudy of legendary World Free Diving Champion Enzo Maiorca, made famous by the cult film classic, *The Big Blue* (portrayed by popular Italian actor Jean Reno).

There were other rumors about Guido to which I paid little attention. Everyone from progressive religious activists to hard-core revolutionaries, along with a seemingly endless flow of "revolutionary tourists" seeking short-term immersion in the latest political hotspot, were to be found nearby in those heady days. Mystery surrounded a good number of the 12,000 *internationalistas* living in Managua and the outlying countryside.

Like many, I dismissed the rumors as fanciful, often meant to enhance the stature of various characters in the cliquish internationalist social milieu.

Rumors and self-promotion aside, there was little exaggeration in Guido's free diving prowess. He approached his craft as a spiritual practice as much as an intense physical pursuit. While it was indeed physically demanding, Guido spent most of his time teaching free diving by counseling me in its mental challenges, a meditative discipline more than a competitive sport.

We started my lessons in a deep volcanic lagoon, Xiloa (a Nauatl/Aztec name pronounced he-lo-WAH), on the outskirts of Managua. The lessons began with an intense breathing regimen reminiscent of the more rigorous yoga disciplines. I would first exhale as long and hard as I could, contracting my lower abdomen upward, then squeezing in my chest, and finally collapsing my shoulders to purge air from my lungs. Then the process reversed as I expanded my lower abdomen, swelled my chest, and took in the last bit of air by lifting my shoulders. All this while I drifted atop the crystal-clear lagoon. I repeated this routine twice before inhaling one more long, deep breath, my blood system flush with oxygen to the point that I began to see bright light sparkling on the periphery of my vision. In only three to four feet of water, I dropped to the bottom and with my dive watch measured how long I could stay under.

I went from holding my breath for a pathetic forty seconds on my first day of lessons to nearly two minutes after several weeks of intensive training. As my breathing capacity grew, we began to concentrate on meditation, with Guido explaining that stress rapidly burned oxygen that would otherwise allow a diver to go deeper and stay under longer. After several more days learning to clear my thoughts and slow my heart rate, I was ready to free dive in earnest.

Early on a Saturday morning, Guido and I swam out into the lagoon where the water was so deep I could no longer see the bottom. After going through the process of supercharging with oxygen, I took that last deep breath and rolled my head and shoulders downward while lifting my legs and fins overhead to create a vertical angle of descent.

My first dive was to a rocky outcropping from the volcanic crater's wall about twenty-five feet down. I set my dive watch at the surface before descending and then went into a vertical plunge. With long, slow scissor kicks I dropped downward at an accelerating rate. Barometric pressure increases rapidly as one descends, and after about ten feet into a dive, buoyancy begins to neutralize. Air in the lungs compresses and causes the descent to accelerate. At around forty feet one's lungs have compressed to less than half their normal size. With buoyancy no longer an issue, drifting at those depths becomes almost effortless.

Guido was waiting on the shelf below, seated cross-legged like a venerable yogi. I came to rest on the shelf and sat across from him. We gazed into each other's eyes as Guido read my demeanor for signs of panic. Once he was sure I was managing my first free dive, he pointed to my dive watch. I gave it a quick glance and realized that less than thirty seconds had passed since I'd set it on the surface. Guido's point was clear—there was no need to stress even if the surface appeared to be far above. Reaching that ledge had taken only a fraction of the time I now knew I could hold my breath. Ascending would be even quicker as the compressed air in my lungs expanded, making me more buoyant as I rose.

My immediate reaction was to grin. Guido grinned back, raising his hands with palms turned upwards as if to say, "See, it's simple." My smile grew wider, which resulted in my expelling air, taking in water, and panicking. I raced to the surface choking and laughing all the way. Guido joined me back on top, laughing as well, then pointed to my watch to make his point yet again. The whole sequence had taken about forty five seconds, less than half the time I now could comfortably hold my breath. The primary focus of training in those early days was to realize that, despite the depth of the dive, one need not stress and unnecessarily burn precious oxygen.

The training process was becoming almost entirely cerebral. The physical elements, while challenging, were becoming easier with each passing day. By the end of the third week, we were diving to sixty-five feet. I found this new sport exhilarating, and I was becoming more physically fit as my lungs stretched and my chest grew stronger. My legs were also getting a workout from powering those long, free-diving fins into the depths. The goal had never been to enter the world of competitive free diving. I had neither interest in nor ability to reach the depths to which true free divers descended. For me it was about the time I spent in near silence underwater, drifting on currents and the tides amongst the magical creatures of the deep. No noisy breathing apparatus or cumbersome tanks used for scuba diving, and no trail of bubbles from a breathing regulator that appeared to fish as if I was one large menacing invader. I could move in this otherwise forbidden world for relatively long periods with little effort as an unobtrusive and nonthreatening presence. It was a time to just be, far removed from the intensity of my journey through the terrestrial world above.

The next weekend the lessons moved to the open ocean. Here I spent most of my time following Guido down into Pacific waters that were not nearly as clear and were colder and often washed by strong currents. I learned to truly appreciate Guido as a master of his element once we were out in open water. He would begin a free dive with his spear gun leading him down. I waited a good thirty seconds before following. When I reached forty feet I would stop and hover in place, searching the seafloor another fifty feet below. Guido would be lying motionless on the ocean bottom behind a large rock with his spear gun resting in front of him like a hunter in his blind. As I ran low on air and returned to the surface, I usually heard a loud THWAP! as Guido fired his spear. I would soon see him emerge from the murky depths with a huge fish on the end of his spear, sometimes nearly as large as he was. As he broke the surface somewhere around four minutes from when he first dove, we invariably greeted each other with grins and laughter. Guido and I spent many days out in the ocean south of San Juan del Sur near the Costa Rican border, sometimes scuba diving, but when the ocean was calm, we much preferred a morning of free diving.

I left Nicaragua a year later to move back to the States and soon lost touch with Guido. I returned occasionally on short work trips but never found the time to reconnect for a day out on the ocean. Nevertheless, I took those lessons with me as I traveled, mostly for work, to various parts of the world, and as often as possible I found spectacular oceans, reefs, and lagoons in which to free dive. From the Caribbean to the Sea of Cortez, the South China Sea to Zanzibar, nearly every trip found a mask and fins in my luggage, and I usually arranged to finish my work assignments somewhere near the sea. After a day of diving, I often found myself reflecting on those bygone days with Guido learning that most wonderful sport.

I returned to Nicaragua in the Spring of 1993 on a short work assignment. A colleague met me at the airport to give me a lift to my hotel. After we exchanged the perfunctory Nicaraguan pleasantries inquiring as to the health of friends and families, we got into her car. Before leaving the parking lot she handed me a folder with the week's work itinerary and background documents, then looked over and asked, "You have heard about Guido?"

I quickly turned to her, a sense of dread rising within me. "No, what happened?" My immediate fear was that he had a diving accident. Free diving is notoriously dangerous, particularly at the depths to which Guido dove.

But she just nodded toward several newspapers folded on the console between us. "I thought you would want to see these." She did not know Guido but knew of our friendship and had often listened to me regaling my colleagues with our free diving exploits. I thought she looked at me oddly, perhaps even suspiciously.

I unfolded the top paper and on the front page ran a story under the title, "Italian Terrorist Hiding in Nicaragua." For a moment I was confused as I began skimming the article. A sinking feeling washed over me as I quickly grabbed another paper, then another, reading rapidly through every story. By the time we reached the hotel I sat stunned, not really responding while my colleague bid me goodbye and quickly drove away.

The newspapers told a sketchy but no less shocking story in graphic terms. Terrorist. Assassin on the run from Interpol. Hiding in the jungles of Nicaragua. Wanted for twelve counts of capital murder, including the assassination of Italian prime minister Aldo Moro. This was an event, I recalled, that occurred not long before Guido and I first met. Some of the stories described Guido in terms reminiscent of the infamous assassin Carlos the Jackal.

The next day, I had meetings booked from breakfast to day's end, but once finished I rented a car and drove the half hour up the South Highway to Guido's house in the hills above Managua. It was just past dusk, and his house was dark. The front entrance was locked, so I rapped loudly with my car keys on the gate's iron frame. The front door opened just a crack. I could not see who it was behind the door, but I thought it might be Guido's wife, Raquel. Before I could speak, she said in a quiet voice, "Guido is not here."

I was not sure what to say, but sputtered something like, "But … what…"

She whispered, "I cannot talk now," and closed the door.

Over the following weeks, I worked through a range of national and international sources, putting together the pieces of a terrible story that left me deeply shaken. Guido's real name was Alessio Casimirri. He was a member of the Italian Red Brigades, an armed ultra-leftist group that emerged at the end of the 1960s when Guido was still a teenager. The Red Brigades were dedicated to sabotage, bank robberies, kidnappings, and had committed more than fifty murders through the 1970s and 1980s.

Their professed goal was to "destroy the capitalist state." The Italian Far Left, like their late-twentieth-century counterparts in much of the Western industrialized world, was enamored with the notion of "armed struggle," celebrating the successes of Cuba, Mozambique, Nicaragua, and other national liberation movements. That such tactics had brought about radical change only in peasant-based and non-industrialized places did not seem to deter the romanticization of political violence as the most effective path to sweeping social change.

Guido, I learned, had participated in the Red Brigades' most infamous crime—the kidnapping and murder of the Italian Prime Minister Aldo Moro. At the time this was the most notorious act of political assassination in postwar Western Europe. Guido (to this day I find it difficult to refer to him as Alessio) was an accomplice in the kidnapping, staging a motorcycle accident in front of the prime minister's motorcade and causing it to come to a halt. Once stopped, other members of the Red Brigades emerged from surrounding cover and ambushed the prime minister's entourage. Five of the prime minister's bodyguards and police escort were killed. According to Italian media sources, Guido was not one of the gunmen, nor was he directly involved in the prime minister's subsequent assassination. Nevertheless, he was tried and convicted in absentia for multiple murders and sentenced to six life terms.

Aldo Moro was one of Italy's greatest prime ministers. The day of his kidnapping he was on his way to parliament to broker the first postwar power-sharing agreement between the centrist Christian Democratic Party and the Italian Communist Party, political rivals since the end of World War II. Had he reached parliament that day, a formalized Historic Compromise would likely have followed, finally marginalizing the still powerful ultra-rightist influences in the Italian political system some three decades after the fall of Benito Mussolini.

Despite widespread popular pressure, Interior Minister Giulio Andreotti would not meet the kidnappers' demand that sixteen Red Brigades prisoners be freed in exchange for the prime minister's release. On May 9, 1978, Moro's captors placed him in the trunk of a red Renault 4, telling him he was on his way to an exchange while covering him with a blanket. Instead, they shot him to death. His body was left in that Renault on Rome's Via Michelangelo Caetani near the Roman Ghetto. The picture of his crumpled body in the open trunk of the Renault remains one of the most searing images of modern Italy, the Italian equivalent of the Zapruder film of John F. Kennedy's assassination in Dallas's Dealey Plaza.

The discovery of Aldo Moro's body on the Via Michelangelo Caetani, Rome.

Not long after the media theater subsided in Nicaragua, Guido was granted asylum due to his marriage to a Nicaraguan woman and his close ties to some of the Sandinista leaders. In another twist in this already complicated story, I soon learned Guido was no longer an actively pursued fugitive by the Italian government. I quizzed an Italian journalist familiar with the case who attributed to "unnamed sources" reports of communication between Guido and the Italian Intelligence Service that led to an agreement not to further pursue his extradition. The journalist believed the agreement was reached in exchange for both information on those involved in "the Moro Affair" and Guido's continued silence about that same information. In Italy, some investigators believed that right-wing elements of the Italian military and intelligence community had infiltrated the Red Brigades, influencing the kidnapping plot and even the assassination to thwart the alliance Moro was about to achieve, but these investigations were all quashed.

Outcomes do not necessarily prove intentions. But Moro's assassination was followed by an end to the negotiations in Parliament over the Historic Compromise. The influence of the Far Right was strengthened within the Christian Democratic Party and broader Italian politics for another decade and a half. The continued power of the Right was accompanied by increased repression of dissent and opposition throughout Italian society.

The story was as complicated as it was confusing. For a time, I repeatedly asked myself, What had I missed in my time with Guido? He appeared to be a good husband and father. He was generous with his neighbors, bringing fish from his diving trips to people who had little access to fresh food in a country under blockade by the United States government. He had become a friend with whom I looked forward to spending adventurous days on the ocean. Nothing seemed to fit or to explain the Guido about whom I was learning. I was left with no answers. I asked a mutual acquaintance how Guido had responded to the charges and uproar around him. She said he denied the stories about him but refused to discuss it further.

Meanwhile, Guido continued to live in relative security under the protection of the Sandinistas. He soon opened, predictably I suppose, the preeminent seafood restaurant in Managua. It was the place to eat and be seen.

More than a decade after being confronted with Guido's hidden past I was once again on a work assignment to Nicaragua, this time as part of an advisory team on a large development project funded by a northern European government. At the end of the assignment, as is often customary, that government's ambassador invited the advisory team, his staff, and several prominent Nicaraguans to dinner at, where else, a popular new restaurant in the hills above Managua called *La Cueva del Buzo*, the Diver's Cave. I thought to myself, *Now this could get interesting.*

Once our group was seated at a long banquet table, the wait staff began to take requests for food and drink. As I looked up to respond to the waitress, I saw her eyes go wide and she exclaimed, "Doooglas!" in that awkwardly charming way that Nicaraguans butchered my first name. It was Raquel, Guido's wife. After a quick hug, she hurried back to the kitchen and a moment later out came Guido wiping his hands on his chef's apron. He grabbed me by the shoulders and lifted me out of my chair, exclaiming in Spanish, "Doooglas! Where have you been my brother?" We embraced, both of us grinning as we always did, as if no time had passed since our last meeting. But in truth, it had been nearly two decades. Guido said we would talk later before excusing himself to return to the kitchen.

As I sat back down, Raquel returned. She instructed that I was not to order a meal because Guido was preparing something special for me. I looked across the table and all eyes were on me, including some stone-faced diplomats and a Nicaraguan vice minister who, with an affectedly demure smile, asked, "So, how is it you are such good friends with Cassimiri, addressing him by his underground name no less?"

It was a long story, I began to explain, but then quickly added as eyebrows shot up, "It had nothing to do with his political history!"

Everyone seemed to let it go. Then Raquel brought a heaping plate of sea bass done in a white wine and lemon sauce that was not on the menu. It was exquisite, and the stares grew stonier.

As dinner was ending Guido reappeared and announced so everyone could hear, "I am going spear fishing to stock the restaurant on Tuesday. I have a new spot you have not seen that has huge fish *en abundancia*! You must come. It will be like old times."

I smiled and stammered in an awkward reply, "Um, I work on Tuesday and then I am going directly back to the States. But maybe the next time I return."

For a moment we locked eyes as we had deep in that lagoon so many years before, Guido reading me as he always did. Then he gave a nearly imperceptible nod and said, "Of course, next time," trying to make the lie we both understood more tenable as he turned and walked back to his kitchen.

The next afternoon I conducted my debriefing for the ambassador and his first secretary as was customary on these advisory missions. It went quickly, with few questions. Then, as was also customary, several bottles of Victoria, a wonderful Nicaraguan beer, were passed around. With raised eyebrows and a sardonic grin, the ambassador observed, "That was quite a reunion last night."

Before he could proceed, I interrupted with a rapid thirty-second summary of my free diving with Guido, at the end of which the ambassador said with a rather magnanimous sigh, "We already know all that. I just wanted to hear you tell it," his smile warming to a wide grin. He then went on to offer that several Europeans, embassy staff included, had taken scuba-diving lessons from Guido over the years, although none had developed quite such a passion for free diving. The ambassador had a sly sense of humor I found decidedly rare among the diplomatic community. His afternoon's entertainment was essentially composed of watching me squirm. Thankfully, he did not prolong my unease for more than a minute or two. He hoisted his beer as a toast and wished me a good flight home. With a long draw on the bottle and a quick nod to his colleague, they both rose and strode out the door. The meeting was unceremoniously adjourned.

This turned out to be my last visit to Nicaragua, but a sense of confusion stayed with me long after. I struggled with my initial desire to understand a friend who appeared to have been involved, I told myself, somewhat marginally in one of the most notorious cases of political assassination in modern Europe. But I couldn't. No matter how I massaged the story of Guido's role and considered the political intrigue and potential manipulation by shadowy interests, this was not an act to be forgiven or excused as the idiocy of a young man caught up in a moment in Italian history. It was an act of extreme brutality that was carefully planned, and it resulted in the murder of six men. Try as I would, I just could not find any other way to understand it.

Over the years, I have followed the repeated, but unsuccessful, attempts to have him extradited to Italy to serve his sentence. To date he remains in Managua, running his restaurant and free diving our old haunts. I have never seen him again. And yet to this day, when I am free diving into some underwater wonderland, Guido sometimes comes to me, not as a terrorist but as an almost mythical creature more at home in the deep blue sea than among land-bound humans such as me.

IV. A Hemispheric Sojourn: Everyday People, Extraordinary Lives

Adulthood came late to many of my generation. I was a case in point. I was forty-three when my son was born, and I was still chasing causes and ideas wherever they led. But parenthood has a way of disciplining otherwise chaotic passions like nothing else. There came a time when I found myself needing to create a more stable and lasting reality for me and my family.

Within several years of my return to the US from Nicaragua, I became a university professor, somewhat to my surprise. For a relatively brief period, I pursued a traditional academic career. I taught, conducted research, and published. It worked out well. The university provided both security and a platform from which I could still indulge my inquisitive mind and restless spirit. I fulfilled the expectations of the academy at an accelerated rate and was promoted through the ranks of the tenured. But it was what that secure post provided me beyond the walls of the Ivory Tower that most shaped my life during my three plus decades as an academician.

Having embraced and succeeded in the "publish or perish" world, I feel little need to reconstruct that part of my life in the following essays. That time is well-documented in the archives of the academy. But my life outside the university walls and my continued engagement in the pursuit of social change was the true measure of my sojourn over these past several decades. Research and development advising were the ostensible purpose of my academic and professional careers. But that undertaking merely allowed me to engage with a range of people whose lives in various ways influenced my own.

It was these people, for the most part relatively unknown and unacknowledged, that led me into and through some of my life's most important lessons. Like me, they were engaged in a quest. Perhaps they have not always recognized our shared journey, but they nevertheless are exemplary of the tens of thousands who defined and carried forward that quest. In the following chapters, I celebrate but a few of the many noble and inspiring folks who helped define my generation.

11. That's the Guy

Acts of conscience are not common, but neither are they rare in the history of my generation. Many of my friends, I have discovered belatedly, made moral commitments during the 1960s and 1970s as conscientious objectors to the Vietnam War. Others made choices that were less widely recognized but no less noble, and some made those commitments at great personal sacrifice. Acts of conscience occurred not only in the United States, and not only against the Vietnam War. They were occurring around the world as a growing sense of outrage over injustice became part of the identity of the post-World War II generation.

In the late 1990s I began working with colleagues at Colorado State University investigating the potential and limits of the nascent fair trade movement as a vehicle for achieving social change. In 1999 we were awarded a grant from the Ford Foundation to bring together the leaders of the movement from around the world. For three days in the spring of 2000, a group of twenty-five participants gathered in Keystone, Colorado, to analyze the movement's efforts to improve social, environmental, and economic conditions among poor, small-scale farmers in the developing world.

On the evening before the workshop, we gathered in a local pub after dinner to get acquainted. I sidled up to the bar and ordered a beer while striking up a conversation with a soft-spoken man about my age named Bob, who I already knew by reputation. He was a driving force behind fair trade in Canada. As was the case repeatedly throughout that gathering, we began exchanging stories about where each of us had been during critical moments in a shared history of political activism. In passing I mentioned that my first trip to Latin America started out in late 1971 as an effort to get to Chile and experience the first socialist revolution achieved through democratic elections. I noted that my trip was cut short by a serious illness, to which Bob responded, "That probably was a lucky turn of events."

I responded by asking him what he meant by that peculiar observation, to which he explained that the coup that put an end to the Chilean experiment in 1973, which happened at the time I likely would have been there, changed many lives, and not for the better. He then, in a near mumble, said, "It had a pretty profound impact on my own."

Quizzing him further, I soon learned a most remarkable story of a decades-long journey that remains an inspiring account of commitment to the pursuit of human rights and the trials one man endured for embracing his beliefs.

In March of 1972, Bob joined the Canadian International Development Agency (CIDA) in the nation's capital of Ottawa as an entry-level project manager. It was a first step on the career ladder of foreign service. Within a year he was promoted. If he continued at this pace, he would likely get his first embassy posting as a third secretary within another year. Family and friends pointed to his achievements with pride. He appeared to be on his way to a career as a development specialist or even a diplomat. Bob had spent two years previously in Peru as a Canadian University Service Overseas (CUSO) volunteer, Canada's equivalent to the US Peace Corps, leaving him with a keen interest in Latin America.

One of the most intriguing developments in Latin America at the time, perhaps the most significant since the advent of Fidel Castro and the Cuban Revolution in 1959, was the 1970 election of Chile's president Salvador Allende, an avowed socialist. To many in the region this was an experiment pursued through "the ballot rather than the bullet," as preceding attempts at radical change had come largely through armed conflict. While the prospects excited some, the new Chilean regime provoked the ire of others, particularly the United States government under then-president Richard Nixon. The United States was steadfast in its opposition to socialist-leaning regimes emerging in the hemisphere, even a democratically elected one. The CIA pursued a variety of covert measures to destabilize Allende's government from its inception. It was only a matter of time before it would lead to crisis.

That crisis came on September 11, 1973, when a faction of the Chilean military, led by General Augusto Pinochet, launched a bloody coup d'état. In the ensuing days and weeks, the military rounded up thousands of civilians, including university students, priests, trade unionists, and others. The capital city of Santiago was locked down as tanks and military patrols swept the neighborhoods in search of suspected Allende supporters. Machine-gun fire echoed through the city day and night. Helicopters thumped overhead as truckloads of soldiers grabbed civilians off the streets, in some cases gunning them down where they stood.

Tens of thousands of people were taken to a large soccer stadium in downtown Santiago that had been converted into a makeshift prison. Prisoners sat in the unsheltered bleachers during the day and slept in crowded rooms, sometimes a hundred to a space where they had to take turns to lie down, all the while awaiting their turn to be taken to a complex of offices and concession stands converted into interrogation chambers. Many were tortured and some summarily executed. An estimated 20,000 people were detained in the stadium in the first months of the coup as a steady flow of military trucks arrived at the stadium each day loaded with prisoners. At night trucks left the stadium filled with bodies or detainees destined for other torture sites from which few returned. Amnesty International reported in December of 1973 that anywhere from 5000 to 30,000 civilians were killed in the first two months. More recent official reports set the number at 3,200 victims. The counting of the dead was hindered by the military and police forces' practice of "disappearing" victims, often dumping their bodies in the streets of Santiago or the Mapocho River that ran through the city. On other occasions prisoners were taken by helicopter over the Pacific Ocean and dumped far out to sea or buried in clandestine graves around the countryside.

When the coup occurred, Bob was in a month-long training program in France. He learned of the atrocities and repressive military measures through daily accounts in *Le Monde* and various Parisian media sources. In Canada, official reports were sketchy, but the networks with links to

Chile, primarily through Catholic priests and bishops as well as through academic channels and unions, kept a steady flow of eyewitness accounts in the Canadian press. Public outcry was growing, with demands that the Canadian government take measures to curb the violence and protect Chilean civilians.

But to the consternation of many, the only action in the initial weeks from Canada's government was to swiftly recognize the military regime as the new legitimate government of Chile, one of the first countries in the hemisphere to do so. As one cartoonist observed in a major daily newspaper, it took Canada twenty-four years to recognize the Chinese government of Mao Zedong, one year to recognize the Cuban government of Fidel Castro, but only eighteen days to recognize Pinochet's military junta.

When Bob returned to Ottawa at the end of September, he went back to the rather mundane tasks assigned to junior-level staff, including filing daily cables between the home office and embassies throughout Latin America. Bob soon grew alarmed at the communications between the Canadian ambassador to Chile and the office of the minister of foreign affairs. What he read was at great odds with what he had learned while in France. In response to questions from the home office about extrajudicial killings, torture, and disappearance of Chilean citizens, the ambassador advised that the Canadian government should not interfere with the new military junta's "thankless" efforts to put an end to Allende's "political madness." The ambassador went on to acknowledge that violent repression was occurring, describing it as both "abhorrent and understandable," observing that the targets of those actions were mostly "the riff raff of the Latin American left." He further offered that Pinochet would soon restore order to the country through these repressive measures, which would be to the longer-term benefit of Canada through its trade and economic ties.

Bob was shaken by the callous disregard for human life. He went home one night and talked at length with his wife. He then sought the advice of a friend about what he had learned. He was consumed with the feeling that he needed to do something. Both his wife and friend counseled him to keep quiet, warning that he was up against the most powerful interests in the country and was putting his career in jeopardy. After a sleepless night he went back to work the next day and made a fateful decision that would irreversibly change his life.

Bob copied several of the telegrams and took them to a member of an opposition party in Parliament. That parliamentarian in turn shared the cables with the press, and then presented them to the House of

Commons. The public outcry was immediate and intense. The tone of the assessment of the situation in Chile was in keeping with the hardline Cold War views held in conservative Canadian circles, believing that any form of socialism, even if it arose through a popular election in a country with a relatively robust democracy, was an existential threat warranting any and all measures to halt it. The traditional popular view of Canada as a defender of human rights stood at odds with the blunt embrace of military brutality as a viable means of eliminating challenges to northern hegemony in the hemisphere.

The ambassador was roundly criticized in the press and in Parliament. Prime Minister Pierre Trudeau and others did not come to his defense, and the public was left with the impression that perhaps he was operating from a personal rather than official perspective.

A senior diplomat from Ottawa and a team from the Canadian Embassy in Argentina were sent to Santiago to facilitate what became a major shift in Canadian immigration policy. The team even went into the holding cells to help prisoners make application for asylum, an unheard-of step in Canada's refugee program. In January of 1974, a Canadian military jet transported the first 137 Chilean asylum seekers to Canada. Where only six Chileans had been granted immigrant status in the year prior to the coup, Canada gradually, then rapidly, increased its acceptance of refugees through the winter and spring of 1974. With the adoption of what came to be known as the Special Movement Chile, Canada eventually admitted some 7000 refugees, an unprecedented expansion of immigration policy toward Chile. A significant number of those admitted were taken directly from their cells, including many from the ranks of the political prisoners awaiting an unknown fate in the soccer stadium. The new Canadian refugee program likely saved the lives of countless Chilean citizens.

In 2013, on the fortieth anniversary of the Chilean coup, the *Globe and Mail*, one of Canada's leading newspapers, ran a feature-length article chronicling the evolution of national immigration policy toward Chile. Almost as an afterthought, in a single sentence near the end of the story, the article observed that the changes in Canada's policy toward Chile had been triggered when classified cables were leaked by an "obscure government bureaucrat." Forty years on, Bob had become little more than an anonymous footnote to a momentous event in the history of Chile as well as Canadian diplomacy and foreign policy.

But Bob's actions were neither obscure nor soon to be forgotten in the eyes of some in his government. The source of the leak was quickly uncovered by the Canadian Security Intelligence Service, and Bob was subjected to intense interrogation and threats from security officials. The minister of foreign affairs called for Bob's prosecution and imprisonment. The demands were echoed by members of the government and Parliament, railing on about his disloyalty to Her Majesty and the Crown.

His immediate family, while not entirely understanding his reasons, stuck by him, as did some friends. Others had strong opinions against him, and still others just did not understand why he would throw away his promising career. Many of his colleagues in CIDA kept their distance out of fear they might jeopardize their careers merely by association. At one point, his hometown newspaper, after listing his family members living in the community by name and address, went on to opine at length on his disloyalty to his country.

With the growing outcry over the human rights violations occurring in Chile and outrage over the initial lack of opposition to the military coup by the Canadian government, the minister of foreign affair's efforts to prosecute Bob were put on hold. He was given the choice to resign to avoid the still strongly held desire by some to put him in prison. He decided to take the offer and left CIDA.

Bob's aspiring government career was over. In time he found work with nonprofit organizations, including the CUSO volunteer service and various church and humanitarian organizations. Much of this work involved short-term contracts without the security government employment had provided. His salary and financial opportunities remained constrained for years after that fateful decision.

In 1984 he was offered a government position in Agriculture Canada, based on his work with rural projects in Latin America. But the offer was soon rescinded when he was denied the requisite security clearance. Thus began a seven-year battle through the Canadian legal system, with Bob challenging not only the intelligence agency's refusal to allow his hiring but also a number of grossly misleading claims about his political views and integrity that had underpinned the agency's justifications for denying his clearance.

After twice winning victories at the appellate court level, the Supreme Court handed down a ruling in 1991 that both vindicated Bob and still left him without a security clearance. The Court ruled that legislation was required to empower greater oversight of the intelligence community at which point the denial of Bob's clearance should be overturned administratively. With that Pyrrhic victory he was left with little hope of ever renewing a government career.

Nonetheless, over the decades, Bob became a progressive presence in both Canada and Latin America through his work with various development projects and organizations, eventually becoming Canada's leading advocate for the newly emerging fair trade movement. In 1998, not long before we met at the workshop in Colorado, he attended a Canadian Steelworkers Union event. Bob was leading a workshop with union activists exploring how the union and the fair trade movement might develop mutually supportive initiatives.

When the meeting broke for lunch, Bob found himself at a table of steelworkers and several nongovernmental organization (NGO) representatives. Across from Bob sat a large man with a shock of black hair and beard, conversing with a woman from a Canadian church organization. Noting the man's rather heavy accent, Bob asked where he was from. He responded, "I am Chilean."

Bob then asked when he had come to Canada, and the steelworker replied, "It was in early 1974."

"Ah," Bob offered, "you were one of the lucky ones."

"Indeed," he replied with an inquisitive look. Then, with a mirthless smile, he went on, "I was picked up and held in the soccer stadium because I was a member of a Chilean trade union. I thought I was going to die. Then some guy leaked a secret telegram. The Canadians came and got me and took me in as a refugee."

Bob just smiled and nodded, saying nothing.

Then the woman sitting beside the steelworker leaned in and whispered in his ear, "That's the guy."

For a moment the Chilean sat there, his brow furrowed, as if he was not understanding her over the din of the crowd. As she repeated herself, a look of comprehension passed over his face. His gaze rose slowly, and his eyes grew wide, locking on Bob's. He suddenly stood, his chair screeching backward and nearly tumbling over. He strode around the table, grabbing Bob by his shoulders and lifting him from his seat. Holding him in a fierce embrace, tears filling his eyes, he whispered in a choked and quavering voice, "Thank you."

Not long after the encounter, Bob was shopping in a Vancouver liquor store. He and his wife were looking for a bottle of wine to share over dinner. While Bob wandered back down the aisle to the wine section, his wife struck up a conversation with the woman behind the counter, asking her for a recommendation. The woman offered that she knew the Chilean wines best since that was her native land. The two carried on a conversation until Bob approached the register. As he placed the bottle on the counter he glanced to his wife who was staring back with a big grin.

"What?"

He looked to the clerk who was smiling as well, but hers was breaking, betrayed by a trembling lower lip. Before Bob could say anything more, the woman came from behind the counter, tears streaming down her face, stammering something in both English and Spanish he could not grasp. In another moment all three were hugging, laughing, and crying, as if in a reunion of long-lost friends.

These encounters were repeated over the years as the small Chilean refugee community came to know who that obscure government bureaucrat was. "That's the guy" has followed Bob ever since, even if its meaning can only be truly grasped by a few thousand people who escaped the horror of a time now a half-century gone.

In 2013 Bob was awarded the Canadian Journalists Freedom of Expression Integrity Award. In typical fashion, he deflected the praise being heaped upon him. He pointed out once again that he had only played a small part as a catalyst in the actions of many people that led to the freeing of Chileans from the grips of the military dictatorship. Indeed, Canadian church groups, academic associations, unions, and human rights activists led a powerful and ongoing campaign that drove the changes in Canadian policy. Nevertheless, that lone act of conscience that forever altered the course of Bob's life, mostly lost in the contemporary narrative of Canada's history with Chile, should not be underestimated, Bob's modesty notwithstanding. In receiving the award, he concluded his acceptance speech simply by offering, "And before you ask the inevitable question, the answer is yes. It was all worth it."

Bob Thomson

12. Connie Stay Home For Peace

It was a harrowing ride up a winding mountain road. Snow-covered peaks towered above us while deep-shadowed canyons plunged away to either side. John Huyler was at the wheel of his sleek blue sports coupe. With the top down, the wind buffeted us as he downshifted through a sweeping curve, then exploded into a straightaway. I sat wide-eyed, clutching the sides of the bucket seat to which I hoped to stay attached. We were on our way to a meeting of political campaigners high in the Rocky Mountains and John was my ride to the gathering. I recalled someone telling me John was once a Navy pilot. I wished I had given further thought to what that casual observation might imply, as it now appeared to be relevant to my continued survival.

Seemingly against all odds, we made it to our destination. Once ensconced in the hotel where the meeting would take place, we moved to the nearby restaurant and continued a conversation over coffee. John is the father of one of my son's closest childhood friends. Over the years I had learned of John's wide-ranging work as an environmental mediator and his deeply held Quaker values. But I knew little of the rest of his life. I thought it might be an opportune moment to learn more about his time as a pilot, particularly because I had yet to make the fateful decision about how I was to get home at the meeting's end. As we chatted I gradually came to realize he was the keeper of a little known story of an amazing action against the Vietnam War, a story begging for the retelling.

In the summer of 1949 four-year-old John, along with his sister and parents, arrived in Ojai, California at the end of a journey from Wyoming in the family DeSoto, trailering two horses and a dog. His father had taken a job as an English teacher at Thacher School, one of the premier preparatory schools in America. It would become John's home throughout his childhood and youth. The family lived in an apartment over a student dormitory. John often took meals in the school dining hall where he sat among students twice his age, listening to and gradually engaging in conversations far beyond the normal reflections of a young boy.

As a teacher's son, John was afforded a free education that only the most privileged and accomplished of the upper class could achieve. The course of study was rigorous. In the summers, John traveled to the Grand Tetons, where he worked on his grandparents' ranch and learned of an entirely different reality from that of classical literature, history, and advanced sciences. Over time, the two worlds grew symbiotic, fostering a confident and adventurous young man.

When John completed his prep school education, he accepted a full scholarship from the US Navy to attend Princeton University, with the condition that he would become a commissioned naval officer upon graduation. His course of study included a traditional university curriculum combined with an immersion in naval science. Once a week he attended classes in the uniform of a Navy midshipman, with his Wednesday afternoons devoted to military marching, drills, and traditions. He spent his summers training in the spectrum of naval warfare, from combat at sea and aerial fighter support strategies to Marine ground combat maneuvers.

When John accepted his scholarship in 1963, he was 17 years old and, in his own words, totally naive about war and what would be expected of him upon graduation. He saw no correlation between his new life and the horrors that were just beginning to unfold half a world away in Vietnam.

But it would not be long before John would arrive at a difficult realization, one many teenagers would come to as the war became an ever greater part of our generation's reality.

John wanted to major in religion. With his grandparents from both sides having been ministers and missionaries, religion was an important part of his intellectual and spiritual development. But the Navy refused his request, explaining they had a well-defined path for recruiting chaplains, and Princeton was not part of that pipeline. He was informed that virtually any other major would do, so he opted for philosophy and pursued the same course of study under a different guise. He studied Gandhi, Thoreau, Jesus, and King, learning of the traditions and ethics of nonviolence from some of the most renowned scholars in American academia.

In the summer of 1964, while John was in Navy midshipman training, a US destroyer engaged several North Vietnamese patrol boats in the Tonkin Gulf. Two days later the same destroyer reported it was again under attack. Subsequent investigations into what came to be known as the Tonkin Gulf Incident found no such attack had occurred. But it set in motion events that would alter the course of American history and the lives of many of our generation, not the least of which was John's. On August 7, the US Congress passed the Tonkin Gulf Resolution authorizing President Lyndon Johnson to dramatically expand the American presence in the region. It was the pretext for launching what would become a devastating and tragic intervention.

John grew increasingly disturbed by the drumbeat of war that was sweeping through the armed services and American society more broadly. He expressed his misgivings to his commanding officers about the military's expectations if he was ordered into combat. He was told in no uncertain terms, if he refused orders or dropped out of Princeton's Naval Reserve Officers Training Corps (NROTC), he would be expelled from the university and immediately begin four years as an active duty enlisted man. Such a move would put him on the fast track to war and the violence he had come to abhor. He found himself in an increasingly untenable position between what had seemed an exciting opportunity and what was quickly evolving into the antithesis of who he was.

One Sunday in 1966 during his junior year, John attended the Princeton Quaker Meeting. He was moved by the simplicity and integrity of Quaker beliefs and began attending Quaker Meetings regularly. It was the start of a lifelong embrace of the Quaker faith. By his senior year, John was struggling with how to continue with both his university education, in which he was thriving, and his military commitments, by which he was increasingly tormented. Meanwhile, he wrote his senior thesis on civil disobedience, and his embrace of nonviolence grew.

As John approached graduation, he informed his commanding officer that he was unwilling to swear that he accepted his Navy commission without reservations, as required in the ceremonial oath of Navy graduation. His commander, by now aware of the transformation John had been going through, advised him to just stand at attention during the commissioning ceremony, and not say anything while his classmates recited their pledge. John thought this would be an acceptable way to navigate the difficult options in front of him while maintaining his increasingly pacificist beliefs. By the ceremony's end, he had not raised his sword, the traditional Navy officer salute, nor had he recited the oath of loyalty. Nevertheless, he was commissioned as an officer and graduated with a degree in philosophy.

By the time of John's graduation in June of 1967, the Vietnam War was raging and John's rejection of any role as a combatant had become clear. John thought he could finesse his way through what he was told was an unbreakable contract by choosing to become a Navy pilot. He reasoned that pilot training entailed an eighteen-month tour at a US base, a length of time he thought surely would outlast the war. To further refine his plan, he opted for training on propeller planes rather than jets or helicopters, the mainstay of the Navy's aerial combat role in Vietnam. At the end of eighteen months John completed carrier landing training and "earned his wings," becoming a naval aviator. But the war had only escalated in the interim, so John volunteered for another eighteen-month stateside tour to become a flight instructor. This, he thought, would undoubtedly be enough additional time to ride out the rest of the war.

At the end of his second tour of duty in 1970, John was sent to San Diego, headquarters of the US Pacific Fleet. His new assignment was to fly a propeller plane towing targets for naval gunnery practice. In spite of spending his days under live fire, he was not engaged in combat nor the killing of others, so he embraced his assignment without hesitancy. He performed his duties conscientiously and was promoted, soon reaching the rank of Lieutenant (O-3), the equivalent of a captain in the other branches of the armed forces.

One evening not long after his arrival, he went to the Quaker Meeting in nearby La Jolla. There he met three men who had been sent to prison for their refusal to go to war. One had refused military service in the First World War, the second during World War II, and the third in the Korean War. As he witnessed the quiet determination with which each man described his experience, John found himself moved by their courage and the strength of their beliefs. Soon after, John and Jim Skelly, another naval officer opposed to the war, drove up the coast to a weekend retreat at the Palo Alto Institute for the Study of Nonviolence. The Institute was the creation of Ira Sandperl, a follower of the teachings of Mahatma Gandhi and mentor to folk singer Joan Baez, anti-war leader David Harris, and many other activists. During the workshop an unnarrated, twenty-minute black and white documentary called *Faces* was shown. Without dialogue, it focused entirely on the faces of Vietnamese children during US bombing raids. John found the terror on the children's faces gut-wrenching, leading him to an irrefutable conclusion: He was done grappling with the contradictions between his commitment and his conscience. Finessing his way through military service was not enough for one who would live by the values he had come to embrace.

At the workshop's end, John returned to base and the next morning informed his commanding officer that he refused to fly for the Navy and had become a Conscientious Objector. John found the officer, not unlike his previous commander at Princeton NROTC, to be thoughtful and caring. He sought to respect John's decision and initiated a process of review with the recommendation that John's decision be accepted. But the Navy brass was not about to let him go quietly. In the fall of 1970, he began a series of psychiatric evaluations followed by a grilling from a panel of three high-ranking Navy chaplains to test the strength and clarity of his convictions. By the end of the process, the reports from his evaluators unanimously concluded John's objections were reached after considerable "spiritual anguish," and based on strongly held religious beliefs. They determined his stance was not one of mere opportunistic convenience and noted that he had performed admirably for over three and a half of his four years' duty as a Navy aviator. The final report recommended he be discharged from the service, and in January 1971, John was granted an Honorable Discharge as a Conscientious Objector.

Rather than availing himself of the opportunity to escape into the anonymity of civilian life, John redoubled his opposition to the war. San Diego was a military town. With the presence of the Pacific Fleet, the local population had an overrepresentation of families and members of the armed forces. But, perhaps not surprisingly, it was also a hotbed of anti-war organizations and activists. Not long after arriving in San Diego, well prior to his discharge, John had begun working with the Concerned Officers Movement (COM). COM was a national organization of military officers who opposed the war but shared a strongly held belief that their best means of expressing that opposition was to remain in the military. COM members argued that they were loyal to their country and the deepest intent of the Constitution. Their commitment, they argued, neither required nor even allowed "blind loyalty." By the early 1970s, COM had grown to 28 chapters across the country with over 3,000 members, including a chapter in the Pentagon. The San Diego chapter became one of the most active and successful in the nation. This in spite of military efforts to stifle COM's presence by transferring members to isolated stations or discharging members with little or no warning. Even after John's honorable discharge, he continued to be an active part of COM's anti-war activities.

John soon became involved in San Diego Nonviolent Action (NVA), a local group that sought to raise awareness among civilians and service members about the nature of the war. NVA declared their efforts were not intended to discredit sailors but were in opposition to the mission into which they had been drawn. The NVA and COM began working together on the Harbor Project, an effort to raise awareness of the critical role of aircraft carriers in the war. By 1970 the ground war in Vietnam was going badly, with growing casualties and ever-more-successful North Vietnamese counterattacks, leading American forces into a strategic shift toward an increasing reliance on attack carriers and expanded aerial bombardment. The Harbor Project was created to challenge the whole foundation of modern warfare as manifested by the attack carrier strategy.

The Harbor Project focused on the USS Constellation, CVA-64, (known within the Navy as the "Connie"), and the project soon came to be known as the Constellation Project. The Constellation was part of a carrier attack group that rotated between the Tonkin Gulf and San Diego on six-month tours, dividing their on-station combat role with the USS Kitty Hawk, CVA-63. The initiative soon caught the attention of prominent anti-war activists, including David Harris. Harris hatched the idea for an action to significantly increase local and national attention on the Constellation Project. He proposed a citywide referendum in San Diego challenging the Constellation not to return to Vietnam. The organizers launched the "Constellation Vote" campaign in the spring of 1971. The plan was to set up ballot boxes around the city and invite the citizens of San Diego, both military and civilian, to cast their vote in favor of or against the Constellation returning to combat in the Tonkin Gulf.

The campaign employed a range of creative tactics the anti-war movement had been successfully using through the latter half of the previous decade. Poster art and fliers were widely circulated, and street theater and concerts became a powerful driver of the campaign. The efforts got a significant boost with a May 15, 1971, *Free the Army (FTA)* performance at a San Diego High School auditorium. Movie stars Jane

Fonda, Donald Southerland, and Peter Boyle, comedian and activist Dick Gregory, and music artists Country Joe McDonald and Joan Baez, joined in the event. It drew a crowd of thousands, including an estimated 2,400 sailors and Marines from nearby military installations.

Campaign organizers followed by circulating a petition among the crew of the Constellation to allow the FTA to hold a second performance on board the carrier. It was envisioned as an alternative to the USO performances on carriers and military bases that began during the Second World War. John could frequently be found in front of the Pacific Fleet base with the FTA petition and leaflets, engaging sailors in conversations about the campaign and the war. The petition drive garnered the signatures of over 1,300 sailors supporting the onboard event.

Predictably, the Navy rejected the FTA shipboard performance. But the Constellation Vote efforts continued. Stickers promoting the vote showed up throughout the Constellation, at one point appearing on the inside of the lid of the commanding officer's personal toilet. Enraged, he went on the ship-wide speakerphone berating the perpetrators, and then ordered the confiscation of all materials coming aboard that he considered subversive. Over 2,500 pieces of First Class mail were intercepted and burned. A protest over the violation of sailors' First Amendment rights ensued, including questioning of whether federal crimes were committed in the destruction of First Class mail. With the unwanted publicity of an official Court of Inquiry hanging over the ship's commander, he was removed from his post.

As the date for the vote drew near, military personnel and San Diego citizens became accustomed to seeing an airplane flying over the city, the harbor, and just offshore of the popular San Diego beaches, trailing a banner declaring "Constellation Stay Home for Peace." It became the iconic symbol of the campaign. The plane was flown by a recently discharged Navy pilot. John was once again throwing himself into the fray with all the resources he could muster.

In late September 1971, the referendum was held over a three-day period. 54,721 votes were cast, with eighty-two percent in favor of keeping the Constellation in port. Seventy-three percent of ballots cast by members of the military were in favor of the same. Nevertheless, the Constellation sailed for Vietnam soon after, although it left without nine crew members. San Diego COM Co-founder and recently discharged Navy fighter pilot Lieutenant John Kent secretly harbored the AWOL sailors while John (Huyler) went from church to church in the local community seeking sanctuary for what came to be known as the Constellation 9. He was repeatedly turned away with claims that the granting of sanctuary had to be discussed and approved within church hierarchy. Finally, John visited a Catholic church in the Hispanic barrio. He was met at the door by a Jesuit priest, Father James Gallo, who within moments of John's beginning to explain the sailors' plight responded with, "But of course." In one of our recent conversations, John reflected upon that moment as the most profound example of unequivocal moral clarity he had ever encountered during his years as an antiwar activist.

John, along with Kent and others from COM and the Constellation Project, camped out in the church with the sailors. The Church made clear it had invoked the ancient practice of Sanctuary. But the military and civil authorities were unmoved. In the middle of the night the church was raided by US Marshalls. The sailors were arrested and immediately flown to the Constellation, where they were locked in the ship's brig. There they began a hunger strike. They became the lead story on the evening broadcast of all three national television networks. After several weeks, the sailors were freed, with all nine granted honorable discharges soon thereafter.

In spite of the Constellation's return to the Tonkin Gulf theater, the Constellation Vote campaign could hardly be considered a failure. It was always a symbolic act, and in that sense it was wildly successful. It raised awareness of the horrors of the Vietnam War, as had many other actions of the antiwar movement. But it particularly focused public scrutiny on the role of Navy attack carriers and the indiscriminate killing visited upon the Vietnamese people. The Constellation Vote marked a significant expansion in the scope of social protest that led to the Stop Our Ships (SOS) campaign to keep warships from departing from bases on both coasts, an initiative that continued until war's end.

John, and many of the other members of COM and NVA, pursued antiwar work long after the fall of Saigon in April of 1975. Like so many others in the anti-war movement, they moved on to other social issues in the decades that followed. John spent much of his career over the ensuing half-century as an environmental mediator, seeking collaborative solutions to contentious issues, often involving local communities facing off against large corporations and government agencies like the US Department of Defense. Now seventy-eight years old, John has become a champion of climate change activism. His latest success came September 29, 2022, when the Divest Princeton campaign in which he played an important role prevailed after a nearly nine-year campaign, with the university announcing it would divest its endowment from ninety fossil fuel companies. John continues to work with Divest Princeton, along with The Friends Committee on National Legislation (FCNL). He has also begun working with The Third Act, an organization of senior citizens engaged in progressive political campaigns while building ties with younger activists.

John maintains regular contact with friends from the San Diego chapter of COM. Referred to as "The Peace Boyz," they meet regularly, most recently for a mid-October 2022 gathering at John's grandparents' ranch. In our last interview, just days before the reunion, John was quick to point out that he should not be thought of as a leader or a particularly notable character in the antiwar movement, suggesting others of his group were far more noteworthy antiwar activists. His discomfort with being singled out is a trait John shares with so many others of our generation. He feels a more collective sense of accomplishment than personal achievement. But that is perhaps the salient point. Many nameless activists led, and continue to lead, lives of principle that eschew recognition. It is precisely their unflagging and often unacknowledged commitment and perseverance that make their stories, and the metanarrative of our generation, so compelling.

From left to right, Norm Bleier, Ltjg USNR, Will Kirkland, Ltjg USN, Paul Rogers, Ensign, USN, John Kent, Ltjg, USN, and John Huyler, Lt USN.

The Vietnam War was a time of awakening for an entire generation. Many young men and women refused to go to war back then, and many more refuse to go to wars since. Many who did go to war joined in the growing resistance. This resistance became a powerful undercurrent in the rise of a generation of protest that engaged with and strengthened everything from the civil rights and Black Power movements, to feminism and national liberation struggles over the past half century. Most of those who resisted the war were working class kids. Young Black soldiers were a particularly powerful force within the military that fostered the growing opposition to the war. But there were others who played an important role as well. Some were officers, and some, like John, were from privileged backgrounds. Together, many people from widely disparate backgrounds built a movement that remains an inspiring example of moral conviction withstanding the most powerful forces of destruction afoot in the world today.

John Huyler

13. By Any Other Name

The Voting Rights Act of 1965 marked a major turning point in the sordid history of racial injustice in America. Not the end of racism by any stretch, but nevertheless a significant moment in the quest for advancing civil and human rights. Meanwhile, halfway around the world, millions of Black South Africans continued to live in a starkly different reality. Confined to shanty towns bordered by barbed wire and controlled by militarized checkpoints, they moved from their townships only with government-issued passes, and then only to travel to work in white-owned factories, fields, and mines. At day's end they returned to their hovels lest they be arrested. No other travel to white-controlled areas was allowed. Voting was prohibited. Marriage outside of rigid racial castes was a crime. Protest was considered treasonous, subject to the death penalty. The 1960 massacre of sixty-nine unarmed demonstrators and the wounding of 180 others in the Black township of Sharpeville, gave harsh testimony to the brutality of the South African regime. It was called apartheid, a white Afrikaner-imposed system of segregation or "apartness." By any other name, it was an unconscionable affront to all the Western world professed to hold dear, a modern-day system of slavery, pure and simple.

The struggle to end apartheid was largely waged in Africa, and while American and European activists played important roles in the campaign, few people today know what transpired within the US that helped bring down South Africa's white minority rule. Following the Sharpeville massacre, the South Africa divestiture initiative gradually became a cornerstone of the international anti-apartheid movement. It was slow to gain traction in the US until a few key activists carried it to the American public. This is the story of one of those relatively unknown actors and the lifelong pursuit of social justice into which the anti-apartheid movement led him.

I met John Harrington in 1983. He had moved to Napa within days of my leaving for college back in the mid-1960s, so while I knew of him for some years, we had never met. I was working at the California Department of Industrial Relations as part of my doctoral dissertation research and earning a professional salary which, after more than a decade of living on graduate student stipends and marginal wages, left me with a modest savings. A friend referred me to John, whom he described as a young investment adviser with an alternative vision to traditional banking and the ubiquitous passbook savings account.

John had recently launched Working Assets as a vehicle for pursuing what was becoming known as "social investing." Over coffee in an East Bay café, he described a strategy focused on companies developing low-income housing or committed to unionized workplaces and rejecting industries like the oil-and-gas conglomerates or the military industrial complex.

John was a warm, easy-going guy about my age who spoke with a disarming southern accent. He had a thick, drooping mustache reminiscent of the Mexican revolutionary Emiliano Zapata, and an air of competence absent pretense. After further reflection, I committed my erstwhile savings to a Working Assets account. In the process, I discovered the remarkable path that had brought John to his new enterprise, and how much he had committed to the broader struggles that were defining our generation.

John grew up poor in rural Texas, living in a one-room house with his mother and grandmother. He picked cotton and other crops throughout his youth and developed an affinity for the Black farmworkers alongside of whom he labored. But he realized early on that while they lived in similar circumstances, a vast chasm stretched between his world and theirs. It was 1950s East Texas, and Jim Crow was alive and well nearly a century after the end of the civil war. A welcome sign stretched above the main street of John's hometown, proclaiming "Greenville—The Blackest Land, The Whitest People." He grew up in a segregated community and attended segregated schools. Those formative years would leave an indelible mark on his conscience.

John led a troubled youth. He repeatedly ran away, fleeing the stifling ignorance of rural southern bigotry. When the New Mexico police sent him home after another failed escape, his mother acquiesced to the inevitable, signing an early enlistment waiver while John was still sixteen. The day after his seventeenth birthday and not yet through his junior year of high school, he enlisted in the US Air Force. He had finally found a way out of his hardscrabble youth.

He became an electrical technician working on B–52 bombers, part of the US Strategic Air Command. The bombers he serviced flew round-the-clock sorties loaded with thermonuclear bombs, the cornerstone of America's Cold War strategy of containing the Soviet Union through "Mutual Assured Destruction," aptly known by its acronym, MAD. He was stationed in Guam for a time where the same bombers flew daily missions "carpet bombing" North Vietnam. Once back stateside, he was stationed at Travis Air Force Base, where he would watch coffins of fallen US soldiers on their final flight home being unloaded from cargo planes. As a nineteen-year-old enlisted man, his insights into US military adventurism were as unique as they were profoundly disturbing.

John was drawn to the anti-war movement early in his military service. In 1965, while stationed at Travis Air Force Base north of San Francisco, he attended a demonstration in San Francisco's Golden Gate Park, showing up in full military uniform. At the rally he was moved by the speech of anti-war activist and California state legislator John Burton. It was a revelation for the young soldier that conventional politics could be used to challenge the injustices he found all around him.

Not long before mustering out of the service, John began taking classes at nearby Napa Junior College. He fell in with a group of progressive students and faculty, volunteering in the legislative campaign of John Dunlap, another local activist, and began doing precinct work in Dunlap's successful campaign for the California State Assembly. John soon became one of a small group of veterans marching in anti-war demonstrations.

John went on to nearby Sonoma State College where he continued his activism. Universities across the nation were becoming cauldrons of protest against the injustices of racism and the Vietnam War. Perhaps because of what he experienced in his youth, John gravitated to the Southern African liberation movements. He found himself particularly drawn to the anti-apartheid campaign in South Africa. He combined his campus activism with his undergraduate studies in economics and political science, writing research papers on the role that US public and private investment played in the burgeoning South African economy.

Upon graduation, John approached Assemblyman Dunlap about working in the California Legislature. Dunlap introduced him to Assemblyman Burton, the same legislator with whom John had been so impressed at the San Francisco rally years earlier. Burton hired John in 1971 and, soon after, John joined the Assembly Office of Research as a legislative analyst. He immediately pressed Burton to draft a report on California's financial links to South Africa, proposing a divestment strategy to help bring an end to the apartheid regime. It was the beginning of a decades-long journey for John that would grow into a relentless challenge to corporate avarice on a global scale.

Divestiture from South Africa was hardly John's brainchild. As far back as the 1950s, church and solidarity groups in the United Kingdom were calling for an economic boycott of South Africa, at the time still part of the British Commonwealth. The Sharpeville massacre catalyzed international opposition to the Afrikaner regime, and divestment became an integral part of the anti-apartheid movement. In 1963 the United Nations General Assembly adopted a resolution condemning apartheid and calling for economic sanctions. Predictably, the Western powers united against the resolution, stifling that and all subsequent General Assembly boycott efforts for decades to come. UK and US business interests were reaping significant economic benefits from continued trade with and investment in South Africa, which remained an overwhelming obstacle to breaking economic ties.

In 1972 John drafted *The State of California and Southern African Racism.* He documented several key dimensions of California's linkage to the South Africa regime, including public pension fund investments in, and state purchases from, corporations doing business in South Africa. John demonstrated how the state of California accounted for upwards of two billion dollars in annual transactions with South Africa, noting that over twenty percent of the California Public Employee Retirement System (CALPERS) funds were invested in companies dealing with South Africa.

Divestiture advocates argued that profit maximization should not be the exclusive driver of investment and business practices, a radical departure from traditional finance culture. The foundational principle upon which traditional investing depended was often referred to as the Wall Street Rule: Vote with Management or Sell—in other words, if a corporation was returning adequate dividends or adequately increasing corporate share value, shareholders should vote their continued support for corporate leadership, or sell. Whether profits were made from the repressive South African government's pass system by Kodak or IBM, as John repeatedly demonstrated, or by supporting Mother Teresa or the Little Sisters of the Poor, should not be the concern of investors. Divestiture introduced a decidedly uncomfortable ethical challenge to longstanding business norms.

John drafted legislation to divest nonvoting shares of pension and other funds' stock from corporations doing business in South Africa, and to use state-owned voting shares to force those corporations to cease doing business with the apartheid regime. The legislation was introduced in the 1973 session by Dunlap, Burton, and John Miller, head of the California Legislative Black Caucus. But the progressive agenda was met with fierce hostility by then-governor Ronald Reagan and Republican legislators, who succeeded in killing every divestiture bill. John was learning what members of the UN General Assembly had discovered a decade prior. While many professed an abhorrence for apartheid, challenging the economic engine at the heart of the modern world economy was another matter altogether.

In addition to rejecting the proposals for divestment, a number of pro–South Africa screeds were leveled at John. Labels like "terrorist" and "communist" were salted generously amongst mainstream media reporting. This was especially true for writings by John McGoff, the owner of the *Sacramento Union*, the second largest newspaper in the region. McGoff was a leading commentator on the divestiture initiative. Some years later, he would be indicted in federal court for being an unregistered agent of the South African government, channeling funds to US media outlets to promote South African propaganda. The indictment would eventually be dropped for failure to meet the statute of limitation requirements.

Some of the attacks on John were based on his contacts with various anti-apartheid groups. He brought representatives from Southern African liberation movements, as well as US-based church and anti-apartheid leaders, to testify during legislative hearings. He also went to Africa to meet with exiled resistance leaders in Dar es Salaam, Lusaka, and elsewhere. On occasion, he met with church and resistance leaders inside South Africa, entering illegally through Swaziland and Botswana. On several occasions he tried entering as part of a tourist group but was stopped and held overnight, during which time he underwent intense interrogations before being expelled.

Far from discouraged, John returned to the fray with a second legislative report, *University of California Investments: Racist or Responsible?* Similar to his previous legislative efforts, he spelled out how public university pension and endowment funds were heavily invested in South Africa, posing a moral question of whether this was an acceptable means of financing higher learning. He bolstered that challenge with a more pragmatic warning, one that would prove prescient—investing in South Africa could one day become a very shaky financial venture.

Soon after the report's release, John was contacted by an attorney for Santa Barbara philanthropist Katherine Tremaine. She was a longtime financial supporter of the Democratic Party and bore the distinction of being on President Richard Nixon's infamous "enemies list." She had read John's report and asked him to advise her on her planned donation to the University of California system, of a hundred acres of prime oceanfront property on the coast of Mendocino County. After extensive discussions with John and university representatives, she notified the University Board of Regents in 1973 that she was withdrawing her donation, based on the university's refusal to divest from South Africa. John arranged for a Bay Area reporter to interview Tremaine. The June 13, 1973, Sunday *San Francisco Chronicle/Examiner* ran a front page story under the banner "Apartheid Issue Hits UC," spelling out the challenge that the donor's action foretold—continued refusal to divest from South Africa was likely to come with increasing financial costs.

But challenging donors had limited potential. Wealthy individuals often made gifts to support wide-ranging priorities, from engineering education to medical research, or to a university's general fund in exchange for naming a building or sports facility. Making divestment from South Africa a criterion for endowment donations more broadly was an uphill slog. Challenging the intransigence of a Republican-controlled legislature, and the similar resistance of university regents and trustees, appeared to be an even less promising tactic.

Instead, John began taking his calls for action directly to the shareholders of companies doing business with South Africa. West Los

Angeles Assemblyman Alan Sieroty, a close friend of Assemblyman Dunlap, gave John his proxy for shares he held in Bank of America. John used the opportunity to address the Board of Directors in their annual shareholder meeting. After spelling out the harsh realities of life under apartheid, John called for halting all loans to South Africa. Bank president and CEO Tom Clausen retorted that the bank would continue to extend loans to any and all creditworthy customers without unwanted criteria, a peevish response that would come to haunt Clausen and the bank in the years ahead. John followed the Bank of America action with shareholder resolutions against Chevron in 1974 and Del Monte in 1976, both deeply involved in the South African economy. While these resolutions were also defeated, John's shareholder insurgency strategy was achieving his goal of raising awareness among an ever-widening audience, some of whom, he hoped, would one day be won over to breaking with the apartheid regime.

John became the "go-to guy" for the divestment initiative within the anti-apartheid movement. He was in increasing demand by organizations and institutions across the country, becoming a regular speaker on university campuses and advising a wide range of anti-apartheid organizations. He worked closely with anti-apartheid leaders, including Dumisani Shadrack Kumalo, director of the American Committee on Africa divestiture project and later South Africa's permanent representative to the United Nations; Prexy Nesbitt, anti-apartheid activist and Chicago community organizer; and other state and national legislators such as Julian Bond of Georgia; Ernie Chambers of Nebraska; and Carol Moseley Braun from Illinois, later a US Senator.

When the Berkeley City Council declared its intention to divest in 1974, John became an adviser to the city's Citizens Committee for Responsible Investing. He provided similar support to the city of Davis and other communities in California and soon expanded that role to other regions of the country. After Jerry Brown became governor of California in 1976, he directed a top economic adviser to enlist John in a plan to reform public pension funds by developing social and environmental criteria for investing public funds. Corporate boards had remained unmoved by divestment resolutions. But public institutions were different in that the governor appointed members of the boards of directors of CALPERS and the California State Teachers Retirement System (CALSTRS). The governor, through his appointees, advanced investment criteria developed by John and the governor's staff that challenged the Wall Street Rule. After more than a year of contentious debates, both public entities began embracing new social criteria to govern future investments.

A year later, Governor Brown appointed John to head the governor's newly created Public Investment Task Force, holding hearings in Northern and Southern California. In the process, John began working with Brown's close allies, Tom Hayden and Jane Fonda, drafting the platform for divestment from South Africa for the Campaign for Economic Democracy. It was a period during which Hayden and his allies nearly wrested control of the California Democratic Party from its historically dominant moderate wing.

By the early 1980s, John's divestiture tactics were evolving. He became increasingly involved in developing viable alternative investment options, including low-income housing, community banks, and other initiatives that generated greater multiplier effects in local communities. John became a driving force behind Socially Responsible Investing (SRI), first through the creation of Working Assets in 1983, then Progressive Asset Management several years later. As president of Working Assets, John regularly traveled to other states and to other countries. He was ostensibly developing his new enterprise, but even a cursory review of his talks and promotional materials reveal that John remained steadfast in his commitment to the South Africa divestiture movement. One early advertisement for Working Assets asked, "Are you banking on apartheid?" followed by an explanation of how Working Assets provided alternatives to traditional banks tied to the Afrikaner regime.

Yet in spite of nearly two decades of unflagging commitment to bringing down the apartheid regime, John's efforts had still produced limited results. It would not be until 1986 that divestment legislation would finally be passed into California law. That same year the UC Berkeley Regents finally acquiesced, divesting $3.1 billion from South Africa, the largest single university divestiture in United States history. It was an action Nelson Mandela would herald a decade later as a turning point in the struggle to end South African white minority rule. UC Berkeley was one of over 150 US universities that had taken divestiture actions by the end of the 1980s.

Similarly, John's efforts with local governments, both in California and across the nation, showed limited results. He achieved a few victories, with the city of Davis passing a 1978 divestiture referendum and the city of Berkeley following suit a year later. But the true impact of that work would also not be realized for another decade. By 1990, ninety cities and twenty-two counties in twenty-six states had taken economic action against the South African regime. Also, by that time over two hundred US companies had cut ties with South Africa, leading to $1 billion in direct South African economic loss. John's shareholder insurgency efforts, like other tactics, eventually achieved major gains, but only after seemingly failing to move the powers that be for more than two decades.

The broader context was also changing. After years of failed efforts, the US Congress passed the Comprehensive Anti-Apartheid Act of 1986, led by Congressional Black Caucus leader Ron Dellums from Berkeley. Then-president Ronald Reagan immediately vetoed the bill. But in a sign of the inroads into public opinion over the preceding decade, the Republican-led Senate split with the president, overriding Reagan's veto, and passing the Act into law. Adopting many of the proposals in the bills John had drafted a decade earlier, the law banned a range of sales, loans to, and purchases from the apartheid regime. It was a major blow to the Afrikaner government. Subsequent congressional legislation in 1987, also led by the Congressional Black Caucus, further tightened restrictions on South Africa.

By 1990, South African inflation was running in double digits, and the South African rand was being steadily devalued as the economy faltered. That same year, in what was the transformative step that sealed the fate of apartheid, the Afrikaner government bowed to international anti-apartheid demands and released Nelson Mandela after twenty-seven years in the Robben Island Maximum Security Prison. The South African government acknowledged what was becoming clear across the Western world, apartheid's days were numbered. In 1994 the white-ruled government conceded to holding the first democratic election in which all South Africans could vote. Nelson Mandela was elected president, and the dismantling of the apartheid regime was at hand.

As Nelson Mandela and the African National Congress undertook the perhaps equally challenging project of building a democratic South Africa, John moved ever deeper into challenging global corporate social and environmental practices. Building on the lessons from his decades-long pursuit of divestiture from South Africa, he engaged retail and computer firms like Toys "R" Us and Hewlett Packard on human rights and labor practices in their sourcing from military-controlled Myanmar. In 1999, he introduced a shareholder resolution at Nike challenging poverty-level wages paid to their Indonesian workers.

Over the ensuing decade he filed seventeen shareholder resolutions at 3COM, Cisco, Intel, Microsoft, Hewlett Packard, and others operating in China, proposing a code of conduct on human and labor rights. He initiated shareholder actions before the Bank of Nova Scotia and the Bank of Montreal, challenging their financing of Canadian fossil-fuel development while calling for consent agreements with Indigenous peoples before drilling and pipelines occurred on native lands.

Now in his late seventies, John is still going strong. He most recently filed a resolution with Amazon, for the fifth time challenging its sale of facial recognition technology used for surveillance of citizens in countries with repressive regimes and by the US government to surveil migrants. He is currently waging a shareholder campaign at Microsoft against its entry into military contracting. While most resolutions continue to be voted down, John remains focused on the long game. Just as the tide turned ever so slowly against apartheid, the corporate human rights and environmental challenges John is waging today may yet reap gains not unlike the divestiture initiatives launched fifty years ago.

The work of John and so many others, while important, should not be seen as having been more significant than the struggles, at great cost, of Black South Africans and their allies within Southern Africa. Nevertheless, John's work to bring down apartheid and his continuing confrontations with corporations on a global scale remain examples of how so many of our generation committed themselves to advancing the pursuit of social justice.

14. A Long Road to Justice

In April 2014, US Immigration Judge Michael C. Horn ruled that former Salvadoran defense minister Gen. Jose Guillermo Garcia not only protected death squads, but also "assisted or otherwise participated in" torture and assassinations.

The arc of the moral universe is long, but it bends toward justice.

Martin Luther King

We met not long after I returned from Cuba. In early 1977 I moved to Santa Cruz to audit classes prior to starting graduate school. One morning while walking across campus, I noticed the announcement of a last-minute addition to the spring curriculum. The course, Comparative Revolutions: The Cases of Cuba and Chile, was to be taught by a graduate student from nearby Stanford University.

The course was perfect, I thought, for addressing my growing disquietude over the revolutionary path of social change. Since I had not yet become an official student, I petitioned to audit the course. Unbeknownst to me, the university had not found a teaching assistant for the course; all the available graduate students had already been assigned. To my surprise, not only was I allowed into the course, but I was offered the teaching assistantship. Given my academic interests in Latin America and having spent a portion of the previous year in Cuba, along with the fact I was already accepted as a graduate student for the coming academic year, I was the best, or perhaps more accurately the only, candidate for the job. So, there I was, being paid to attend the class I most wanted to take.

On the first day, Terry walked briskly into the classroom and up to the podium. She was short, not even five feet tall and probably no more than a hundred pounds, her small stature only slightly augmented by her "Jewish afro." She looked like the undergraduates gazing up from the desks in front of the lectern. But any resemblance to a young student disappeared as soon as she set about explaining the deep and challenging questions upon which the course was based. Successful revolutions were as complicated as they were rare, and these two cases would make that abundantly clear.

She then explained her expectations of those who decided to return after the opening session. The reading was extensive. Testing would involve several essay exams and a term paper, with all the expectations of scholarly conventions included, along with weekly small group breakout sessions in which students would demonstrate their grasp of the readings and lectures. It all added to the sense that this was going to be no ordinary course and that passive consumers looking for an entertaining, and not-to-demanding course, were not likely to fare well.

The course turned out to be everything I had hoped. Terry was a gifted teacher. Her lectures, often drawing on her extensive field work in Cuba and elsewhere, were spellbinding, and she soon became the talk of the Latin American Studies Program. When the ten-week quarter ended, she immediately disappeared into Venezuela to pursue her dissertation research while I started graduate school several months later.

In the ensuing decade, Terry and I became fast friends. We found ourselves increasingly sharing interests around the dramatic changes sweeping Central America. As the years went by, we supported and encouraged each other through the trials and tribulations of our careers, of major health challenges, a successful, albeit career-altering, sexual harassment suit (Terry, not me), and more. When my son was born, she became his godmother. Over what is now four and a half decades since we met, I have followed her unwavering pursuit of social justice, a pursuit that more than once put her in personal peril. I offer her story here as another inspiring tale of my generation's quest to change the world.

Terry went to El Salvador in 1981. At the time, she was an assistant professor of government at Harvard University. Just prior to her arrival, the archbishop of San Salvador, Óscar Romero, was assassinated while giving Sunday Mass. He was targeted for his calls to end the violence and embrace a peaceful reconciliation to the brutal civil war ravaging the country. Soon after, three American Maryknoll nuns and a lay worker were murdered by Salvadoran National Guardsmen.

Immediately upon her arrival, Terry was confronted with the horrendous reality into which she was venturing. She encountered the mutilated body of one of the death squad victims alongside the highway as she traveled from the airport to the capital. That same night, she quite literally stumbled upon the body of another victim in a McDonald's parking lot next to her hotel. If she was not fully prepared for the savagery of the Salvadoran civil war, then neither would she be deterred from her investigation.

Prior to her arrival, Terry had been working on a book about the destabilizing impact of oil booms around the world. It was to be her first major scholarly achievement, with a tenured Harvard professorship her potential reward. Once in El Salvador, she quickly set that project aside to focus on researching the sources of the violence and the possibilities for bringing the seemingly intractable conflict to an end.

Several nongovernmental organizations (NGOs), especially the organization now called Human Rights Watch, were already documenting the hundreds of civilian murders occurring daily throughout the country. Terry took an alternative and riskier path. While she interviewed people from across the political spectrum, much of her time, and many of her most revealing insights, came from interviews with far and center-right military and civil society figures. She soon learned they gave no quarter, intending to kill or terrorize anyone they deemed part of the opposition. That was particularly the case for the powerful, and unarmed, center and left political parties like the Christian Democrats. But their willingness to torture and murder went far beyond, to include the rural poor, students, Catholic priests, and others. They were all deemed "likely" communists because of their opposition to the century-old political order.

She traveled with the ultra-rightist ARENA party leader Roberto D'Aubuisson on his presidential campaign to learn more about that faction of the ruling elite. He would later be named in a United Nations investigation as one of the "intellectual leaders" behind the death squad responsible for the assassination of Archbishop Romero. She went on to interview members of the Left as well, including the leaders of the Frente Farabundo Martí para la Liberación Nacional (FMLN).

Terry pieced together a profile of the range of actors and the dynamics at play in the Salvadoran civil war. Given the danger to not only herself but those she interviewed, she never recorded her meetings and was careful to write her notes in a code only she could decipher. And with good reason. She was being followed. Her hotel room was searched repeatedly while she was in the countryside conducting interviews. It was apparent she was getting closer to things others thought best kept unknown.

In December 1981, not long after her initial visit, the Salvadoran military carried out the largest mass killing in recent Latin American history. Known as the El Mozote massacre, nearly one thousand rural peasants were killed in a two-day military action, 533 of them children under the age of fourteen. It would become the most notorious massacre of the civil war, but far from the only case. Salvadoran activists, along with Terry and others from the international community, would document many more massacres in the ensuing decade.

The Reagan administration, through Assistant Secretary of State Elliot Abrams, vehemently denied the massacre had occurred. Where evidence of mass murder and torture were beyond even their denial, the administration blamed leftist rebels or rogue elements within the military. At the same time, the administration assured Congress and the American public that progress was being made toward ending the atrocities and establishing a peaceful democracy.

Drawing upon her findings and those of the various Central American investigations, Terry became increasingly active, giving talks in the US and elsewhere on the unfolding horror. Her research fundamentally contradicted the Reagan administration's narrative. Back at Harvard, she began drafting reports for congressional Democrats opposing administration policies. Over time she also succeeded in convincing several well-known Republicans about the true nature of the Salvadoran violence. Nonetheless, efforts to cut off aid to the Salvadoran military were steadfastly resisted by most congressional Republicans and the White House.

Roughly twenty percent of the Salvadoran population fled the country during the civil war, many of them finding their way to the United States. With the Reagan administration's downplaying of the violence while claiming the country was becoming a viable democracy, Salvadorans who had reached the United States faced enormous challenges proving their petitions for asylum. Terry wrote hundreds of lengthy affidavits in support of political refugees and often appeared in court to give testimony in asylum cases, all *pro bono*.

In the early morning hours of November 16, 1989, a unit of the Salvadoran military's Atlacatl Battalion, an elite counterinsurgency force trained at the US Army's School of the Americas and implicated in the 1981 El Mozote massacre, entered the Central American University. They pulled six Jesuit priests, a housekeeper, and her sixteen-year-old daughter from their beds and murdered them. Among the priests was Father Ignacio Ellacuría, rector of the university and an internationally respected theologian. He was also a leading advocate for a peaceful settlement to the civil war.

The murders brought unprecedented outrage from around the world. Salvadoran president Alfredo Cristiani was quick to blame the rebels for the murders, as had been done previously in response to the El Mozote massacre. But the attempts at deflecting responsibility had by then become widely recognized for what they were: cover-ups. The murders represented a personal tragedy for Terry as well. She knew three of the murdered priests, including Father Ellacuría, and had organized a research collaboration with them at Stanford University to document the growing violence and repression.

The Jesuit murders were a turning point in the Salvadoran conflict. The repressive rulers of the country knew a change in their fortunes was coming. As the Berlin Wall fell, newly elected president George H. W. Bush backed away from his predecessor's hardline commitment to the Salvadoran military. In 1990 the United Nations Assistant Secretary General convened negotiations between the Salvadoran government and the rebel forces. Over twenty months, a series of agreements were hammered out, culminating in the Chapultepec Accords of February 16, 1992, in Mexico City, bringing the civil war to a formal end. The commission included a number of Latin American leaders and international experts. Terry was among the peace process advisers.

Soon after, again under the auspices of the United Nations, negotiations were revived for a peace agreement in Guatemala, El Salvador's northern neighbor. In 1996 a comprehensive agreement was finally reached, bringing an end to the most violent of all conflicts in the history of the region. With former Costa Rican president and Nobel Peace Prize laureate Óscar Arias, Terry co-chaired the initial session of the peace agreement process.

Through it all, Terry's more traditional academic career flourished. She left Harvard in the mid-1980s and joined the political science department at Stanford University soon after. Her academic work, while including writings on human rights and democracy, primarily focused on the politics of oil. She also became a widely celebrated teacher at Stanford, winning virtually every university award for pedagogy. In 1997 she published her long-delayed book, *The Paradox of Plenty: Oil Booms and Petrostates.* She became the first scholar to demonstrate how oil booms, and the influx of wealth they generated, destabilized democracies, strengthened authoritarian regimes, and led to wars. Her book became a classic. Ten years later the March 14, 2008, cover of *Time Magazine* ran a headline, "10 Ideas that Are Changing the World." The "paradox of plenty" was one of those ten ideas.

Over the ensuing decade, Terry's academic research took her to Europe, Africa, and the Middle East. But she could not forget the human rights crimes she had witnessed during the years of the Salvadoran civil war. In 1999 she was approached by attorneys from a newly created NGO, the Center for Justice and Accountability (CJA). The attorneys were developing a new strategy to confront the impunity with which individuals and organizations carried out their crimes. Terry immediately agreed to become the lead researcher and expert witness in the innovative legal initiative.

Since the Second World War, the United States has been a haven for civil and military leaders from authoritarian and dictatorial regimes. Terry worked with the CJA legal team to develop new ways to use US civil law to charge foreign nationals living in the US with war crimes and human rights violations. The initiative was aided by a list compiled by human rights groups and others, of roughly one thousand individuals living in the US who were suspected of war crimes.

El Salvador became the starting point for a legal initiative that would have far-reaching implications. With her detailed knowledge of the processes and individuals at play in the civil war, Terry became critical to this evolving effort. Her research got a major boost by then-president Bill Clinton's release of thousands of pages of previously classified documents from the State Department, Central Intelligence Agency, and others. The documents were a treasure trove of data providing extensive details of the Salvadoran military's brutality, as well as the Reagan administration's knowledge of, and complicity in, the cover-ups. Terry spent two and a half years analyzing and compiling evidence that culminated in the trial of two former Salvadoran military leaders, José Guillermo García and Carlos Eugenio Vides Casanova.

Vides Casanova was in command of the Salvadoran National Guard at the time of the murders of the Maryknoll nuns and was minister of defense during other atrocities. García was minister of defense at the time of the El Mozote massacre. Both had left El Salvador in 1989 when it was clear the civil war was drawing to an end. García was granted political asylum and Vides Casanova a Green Card. They had been living in the Miami area ever since. CJA filed a civil suit in the Southern Federal District Court of Florida against the two generals. Three Salvadorans living in the US who were victims of torture at the hands of the military became the plaintiffs in the lawsuit, *Romagoza Arce v. García and Vides Casanova.*

Terry's research helped develop what came to be known as the "doctrine of command responsibility," based on principles established in the Nuremburg trials at the end of the Second World War. The principle of command responsibility had never been applied in US legal proceedings regarding a foreign conflict. She demonstrated that the many murders, tortures, and other atrocities could not have been perpetrated without the direct knowledge or tacit approval of the two military leaders. She further argued that both leaders were part of the *duros* or hardline leadership of the military that embraced a commitment to brutal repression of any opposition to military rule.

Terry's task as an expert witness was to explain the nature of the civil war and the complete control military leaders had over the actions of soldiers in the field. The jury was made up of West Palm Beach citizens who knew virtually nothing of the Salvadoran conflict, nor in many cases, even where the country was located. Nevertheless, jurors were spellbound by Terry's testimony, offering in posttrial interviews that she had been decisive in their decision to rule on behalf of the plaintiffs. On July 23, 2002, after a four-week trial, the jury found the defendants responsible for the torture of the plaintiffs. The jury awarded the defendants 54.6 million dollars. Based on that ruling, the CJA team, working with Homeland Security and the US Immigration Service, pursued further legal action against the generals that culminated in their 2016 expulsion from the US.

The Romagoza case set in motion a significant shift in US government legal policy. It led to new law allowing for the deportation and/or extradition of perpetrators of war crimes from the US if they could be shown to have committed crimes in their home countries. The doctrine of command responsibility became a cornerstone of this new policy.

As the case drew to a conclusion, CJA found another Salvadoran perpetrator of human rights crimes in the US. Álvaro Rafael Saravia was living in Modesto, California. He had left El Salvador in 1990. Saravia was the security chief of death-squad leader Roberto D'Aubuisson, whom Terry had interviewed two decades earlier. In 2003 *J. Doe v. Álvaro Rafael*

Saravia et al. was filed in the US Eastern District Court of California on behalf of one of Archbishop Óscar Romero's relatives. Saravia disappeared when an attempt was made to serve him with a subpoena. In his absence, the case continued. Terry again was the expert witness providing detailed and convincing evidence linking Saravia to Romero's assassination. In 2004 the judge ruled in favor of the plaintiffs. It was the first time in US legal history that the killing of a single individual, the archbishop, was ruled a crime against humanity. The evidence Terry provided is now the basis for a case recently filed in El Salvador.

The new legal strategy gained increasing traction among legal activists, and the demand for Terry's unique skillset grew. She worked for both government agencies and NGOs. Three cases in particular demonstrate the advances in pursuing war criminals and human rights violators that resulted from this legal strategy. The first was the case of Colonel Nicolás Carranza, former vice minister of defense, and later director general of El Salvador's treasury police. The treasury police were notorious for torture and murder during the civil war. Carranza moved to Memphis in 1985 and became a naturalized citizen. A civil suit was filed on behalf of several torture victims and family members whose relatives were murdered or disappeared by the treasury police. Terry's testimony was again key to convincing a jury of Carranza's culpability. In 2009 the court awarded a six-million-dollar settlement to the plaintiffs. During the trial Carranza, who came to be known as the "Eichmann of Memphis," revealed that he was a paid CIA informant. Perhaps because of that, Carranza remained in the US, in spite of the court ruling, until his death in 2017.

In 2011 Terry began working with several Spanish human rights organizations to bring charges against twenty members of the Salvadoran military for the murders of the Jesuit priests, several of whom were Spanish citizens. In August of 2011, Inocente Orlando Montano Morales was found to be living in Massachusetts. Montano was the vice minister for public safety at the time of the murders and present when the order was given to "eliminate" Father Ellacuría and make sure there were no witnesses.

Working with the US Immigration Service and the US Department of Justice, Terry provided evidentiary affidavits that helped make the case against Montano on charges of immigration fraud and perjury. After a lengthy legal battle, Montano was extradited to Spain in November of 2017. Terry followed Montano to Spain and provided critical testimony in Spanish court that resulted in Montano's September 2020 murder conviction. He is now serving a 133-year sentence in a Spanish prison. To date, he is the only high-ranking Salvadoran military leader to be imprisoned for the civil war crimes.

Terry's pursuit of human rights violators took another turn in 2016 when a 1993 Salvadoran amnesty law was struck down by the Salvadoran Supreme Court. Since its adoption, the amnesty law had made it impossible to prosecute perpetrators of the atrocities committed during the civil war. With this opening, Terry began working with prosecutors and the only judge in El Salvador willing, or brave enough, to hear a case against El Salvador's military high command. They went after the leaders behind the infamous El Mozote massacre, among them General José García, the same General García Terry had just helped expel from the US.

In the summer of 2021, Terry became the first "*gringa* expert" in a human rights case inside El Salvador. She spent three days on the stand giving testimony against General García and the military leadership. The courtroom was packed with families of the victims of the massacre, along with members of the press and diplomatic corps. With Terry proceeding methodically through the evidence, the case was seemingly overwhelming. The noose appeared to be tightening on the Salvadoran generals.

But in what has been described as a "judicial coup," Salvadoran president Nayib Bukele Ortez intervened the day after testimony concluded, and before a ruling could be reached. First, he replaced all five judges on the Supreme Court. Then, in a patently unconstitutional maneuver, he retired all judges over the age of sixty. It was an action that more than coincidentally included the one judge willing to preside over the El Mozote trial. With a new Supreme Court handpicked by President Bukele, the removal of the trial judge was upheld, effectively ending the prosecution. For the moment, bringing General Garcia to justice was not to be.

Several months after the abrupt end of the trial, I called Terry as I was about to write this memoir. I asked if she was feeling discouraged or like it was time to just ease up a bit. "We're about the same age," I noted, "and I for one cannot deny I am feeling the weight of time."

She replied, "I am not at all discouraged. For one, they can no longer deny the role of the Salvadoran military in the El Mozote massacre, or many other crimes against humanity. As for carrying on, I can't have spent all these years with those wonderful and proud people, with the mothers of the victims of El Mozote or the priests who persevered through the terror, and now turn away. I have already begun new research to prepare for more cases."

As I write this memoir, the horrors unfolding in Russia/Ukraine, in Gaza/Israel, and in other less-well known parts of Africa, Asia and beyond, are heartbreaking reminders that until we put an end to the impunity with which perpetrators of crimes against humanity carry out their misdeeds, we will undoubtedly witness continued and even escalating human suffering. While justice appears as fleeting as it is difficult to achieve, it is hard to imagine that peace will ever come without it. It is people like Terry who give me hope that we will one day hold evildoers accountable, and in so doing come closer to the time when such barbarism is relegated to a dark and distant past.

15. The Blessing

A childhood acquaintance, David Two Bears, a practitioner of his Chiricahua spiritual traditions, sent me an email a couple of days ago. He said he had been thinking of me and asked if I would accept a blessing that day while he was "of the spirit." I had been corresponding with David over recent months about a couple of memoirs I had written. I was enjoying reminiscing and learning of his life since we last crossed paths well over a half century ago. I responded to his offer with gratitude and was about to observe that I had never been honored with a spiritual blessing in a native tradition. But then a magical morning in the Chiapas highlands some three decades prior came flooding back into my memory. I have thought of little else in these past few days and have put down here that haunting experience in the hope it will never escape me again.

In 1990 I accepted a visiting scholar post at Stanford University's Center for Latin American Studies. Several months earlier I had been awarded a MacArthur Foundation Research and Writing Grant to write a book on the health crisis caused by chemical-intensive farming in Latin America. About a year into my stay, I was asked to assist a Stanford Medical School health project underway in the highlands of Chiapas, Mexico. My book project was going well, and exploring a new region of Latin America was an intriguing diversion.

In early 1991, I joined a team of medical researchers working in the village of Navenchauk, a Tzotzil-speaking Mayan community of about 4000 people. The researchers had encountered problems trying to include the entire community in a health assessment. Along with a Stanford anthropologist, I was tasked with identifying the obstacles to greater community participation and developing a strategy for getting the initiative back on track. The anthropologist—known as George by everyone with whom he worked and as Jorge by locals throughout the region—was a renowned scholar of Chiapas culture and history who spoke the local dialect. My experience with community health projects in other parts of Latin America was deemed an additional resource, although I confess I had far less to offer than George.

The primary obstacle to more complete community participation became apparent relatively quickly, although it appeared to have escaped those leading the effort. The researchers had entered the village with the assistance of an English-speaking Mayan interpreter who had in turn hired several villagers to facilitate the project. Predictably, at least in hindsight, the village assistants were all from the same family lineage and religion as the project's interpreter. While Navenchauk appeared to be a homogenous Mayan community of the Zinacantan region, it soon became clear it also had a significant minority group with a different family lineage and a distinctly different religious tradition.

As we talked with the local team, we learned that in their view they had obtained the participation of all the members of the community. That a significant minority of the community residents were not participating elicited a simple response—those people were not members of the community. The fact that this minority group still lived in the village seemed to be only an inconvenient and irrelevant fact to the local team. The solution, neither simple nor quickly achieved, was to create a second team of assistants from the minority group to facilitate the participation of the remaining residents.

To set the new strategy in motion, George and I, along with one of his graduate students, went to meet with a village elder to help gain access to the remaining community members. He had offered to meet us at first light at a simple thatched-roof, mud-and-wattle hut in his small family compound near the edge of Navenchauk.

It was cold and damp; patches of fog hung low over the surrounding hills. George was dressed in traditional Mayan attire, a broad-brimmed straw hat, an embroidered poncho worn over a white cotton long-sleeve shirt, and white cotton pants that reached to just above his ankles, along with the ubiquitous huarache sandals. In keeping with ceremonial traditions, the elder brought a jug from his hut and filled a small clay cup with a clear liquid, a potent locally distilled alcohol called *pox* (pronounced "posh"). The first cup was offered to George in keeping with his revered status. He tossed it back in a single motion. Then the cup was refilled and offered to me.

Since the village was some distance from where we were staying in San Cristobal de las Casas, we had risen and left nearly two hours before daybreak, without breakfast. I followed George's lead and drank down the ritual offering, and it hit my throat and stomach like a red-hot branding iron. But in keeping with George's example, I swallowed, caught my breath, smiled, and thanked the elder. Also in keeping with indigenous tradition, the graduate student, a young woman in her late twenties, was offered the last full cup which she drank without grimace or gasp, eliciting a grin and a nod of approval from the elder. We had now been properly received and ready to begin the day's task.

But rather than enter into a discussion of how to proceed with the project, the elder explained that there was a crisis developing in a village over the nearby hills, a smaller community called Apas. He did not explain the nature of the crisis but said that we must go there directly and lend a hand. I did not understand what it was we were expected to do, but George just nodded and replied, "Of course." Without further discussion we set out along a narrow footpath up a steep slope still shrouded in dense, swirling clouds.

Climbing through largely deforested hills marked intermittently by eroded farming plots now abandoned and no longer fertile, we met a Mayan man of indeterminate age, descending on the path back toward Navenchauk. We walked single file with George in the lead, his head downcast in keeping with local custom. As we passed, George, in an almost imperceptible whisper, greeted the man in his native dialect. He did not look up nor otherwise acknowledge the passerby. When the villager drew alongside me as next in line, he looked up with startled confusion, and then broke into a wide grin as he looked back at George. He was clearly surprised by the Anglo dressed in traditional garb who greeted him in his ancient Mayan tongue.

We walked on for another hour until we crested a summit. Below us was a small village. To one side at the top of a rise was a long, low, cinder-block building with a roof of red-clay tiles. A gathering of several dozen women and children sat or stood in small clusters outside the building, talking in hushed whispers. They were dressed in their most colorful attire, indicative of an important event. As we approached, we were fixed by their unwavering gazes, stern and dark, neither curious nor hostile. It felt as if we were simply irrelevant to whatever momentous event had brought them to this promontory.

Inside the building, rays of sunlight tunneled down through the smoke-filled interior from gaps in the tiled ceiling. As we approached, two elderly men, dressed in elaborately embroidered ponchos and ceremonial hats, stepped from the dark interior and greeted us in their native dialect. George and the two elders began conversing in low tones, their heads bowed close together as if reading from an invisible script hidden in the dust at their open-sandaled feet, their serious expressions never changing. The conversation went on for the better part of a half-hour as first the elders spoke at length, then George responded in a long, slow soliloquy, followed by shorter exchanges of what I thought might be questions and answers. Then the two elders gestured for us to wait as they turned and reentered the building. We could hear one or more men addressing a group we could now see seated on long, low, wooden benches around the interior walls. At times there was silence followed by what seemed formal orations. Voices never rose nor fluctuated to give any sense of emotion or discord.

The two elders George had engaged in conversation now more than an hour past, exited the building again. One motioned for us to follow, and they turned back through the open doorway. We stopped just at the threshold as the elders came about to face us. Looking inside, I saw that it was a long, single room meeting hall. It appeared to double as a church as there was an altar at the front of the room. There were several clay bowls smoldering with incense near the altar. The hall was clouded in near-choking acrid smoke, creating a swirling and shadowy haze. As we stood there, the older of the two men spoke a slow incantation. George kept his head bowed while the graduate student and I watched without knowing what our role or behavior should be. Then George looked up and nodded to both men and turned to us. In a barely discernable voice, he gestured toward the trail back down the hill and said, "Time to go."

We walked away in silence. Once we were some distance from the gathering, we stopped and sat on a large rock outcropping next to the trail. George gave us a rundown of what we had just witnessed. The gathering had been called by the head of the community after one of the elders had returned from a trip to San Cristobal de las Casas. He had watched a television newscast with a scene of the carnage of war. George began to explain that it was only after some time in his discussion with the two men, one the village headman and the other its curandero or shaman, that he realized they were referring to a newscast portraying the war in Iraq. The man who watched the broadcast knew nothing of the Iraqi War, but what he saw left him shaken. He saw bodies strewn along a roadside among burning vehicles as a column of light-skinned soldiers who he assumed, correctly, were Americans, marched slowly by. The bodies were all dark-skinned and dark-haired men and boys in tattered clothing that looked to him ever so much like his own people.

He concluded the obvious. The Americans were coming from the north to wipe out the indigenous people of his homeland. His sense of where the conflict was occurring, and where the invading Americans were, was based on a different sense of geography, of distance and time, of the world in its entirety. I had experienced this difference numerous times over the decades that I had lived and worked in rural and indigenous places. On many an occasion a peasant or indigenous person who had not likely traveled more than a short distance from their community in their entire life, would point to the mountains on the farthest horizon and explain to me that a distant event, wherever I might understand it to be occurring, was on the other side of those mountains. "*Más allá*" they would say, "beyond there." That was their spatial scale of reference. Their temporal sense was equally as different from mine, which often left me totally confused as to where or when, or even what, we were discussing.

We sat in rapt attention as George went on to explain what we had not only just observed, but participated in. The reports of impending invasion seemed to validate other rumors among the community. The village elders, after meeting and debating what it all meant, sent out a call to all the village members, including those who had moved to other communities and regions. They set a date when the entire extended community was to gather. The gathering would be a ritual to celebrate their people and embrace the impending doom that was about to befall them. That was the ceremony we had come upon that morning.

George described how he had offered his own interpretation of what the villager had witnessed on television, explaining that he had heard stories different from those the villager had heard. The Americans were indeed at war, but the conflict was occurring in a place much further away. He explained that the stories he heard told of a conflict nearing an end, and that the soldiers would soon return to their homeland. He offered that he had not heard they would be coming to the Chiapas highlands.

I was struck by how careful George was not to offer information as if he was the authority on these matters, but instead consciously constructed his impressions as stories he had been told, just as the elder and others had offered their stories. He seemed to be very careful not to convey his truths as somehow more valid than theirs, but instead as alternatives to be weighed, accepted, or rejected, as the elders decided.

The village leaders had shared George's interpretation with the gathered community members. They had discussed it and offered incantations to their ancestral deities, in particular the gods of the earth to whom they looked for protection. The shaman had then, after inviting us to approach the threshold of the ceremonial hall, performed a blessing upon George, and us by association, for having been sent as the bearers of useful stories in a moment of great darkness.

I sat there on that rock beside the dirt path winding back down the hillside, shaking my head in wonder. So many thoughts to sort out. This seemed to me a moment of total culture clash as late twentieth-century technology came up against a centuries-old culture at profound odds with the modern Western world. Even as international communication was occurring just a couple hours away, this somewhat remote community, still without electricity and other industrial-world amenities, was going about their lives less influenced than I would have assumed.

Then I reflected on what those villagers were experiencing that morning through their lens on reality. They had come together to both celebrate their families and community, and to say their farewells before the onslaught from the north overwhelmed and exterminated them. The nobility with which they gathered in stoic solidarity rather than the abject terror one might otherwise expect brought tears to my eyes.

I left Chiapas soon after and forgot about that morning's encounter for another thirty years until I received David Two Bears's offer of a Chiricahua blessing. The memory his offering triggered started me reflecting upon my original impressions about the misunderstandings that grew out of the clash of a more technologically developed world with that of a centuries-old and very different system for interpreting reality. It occurred to me that my initial perception of that morning on the hilltop overlooking Apas was narrowly framed by my own sense of the universal validity of Western modernity. It occurred to me that if I stepped back and revisited that ceremony and thought of the impending doom they foresaw in a more metaphorical way, then they might have indeed been accurately predicting a fate that is befalling them with ever-greater severity.

With each passing year, the modernization from the north has been challenging and invalidating the belief systems and practices of this ancient Mayan culture. Their communal lands are shrinking through privatization and land grabs. Their farmlands are being degraded by overcultivation and climate change, intensified by a roughly forty percent population growth in these past three decades. Their foretelling of extermination at the hands of invaders from the north, metaphorically, may hold more truth than my "modern" thinking could grasp.

This renewed reflection has left me questioning more deeply, and not for the first time, whether my Western worldview might not be the only "valid" or "accurate" interpretation of reality. To band together in ceremony, to celebrate ties that one day, maybe soon, will be gone, seems perhaps more enlightened than the obsession with individualism, linear time, a science-defined reality bereft of enchantment, and a "manifest destiny" that pervades the American identity. There is more to these reflections, I know. I am looking forward to exploring them further, and, if I am so fortunate, to embracing what future blessings come my way.

V. Conclusion: The Quest Continues

We make our history out of what we choose to see in the past.

Thomas Dyja

Our generation, or at least the minority of seekers who came to define it, were dreamers and experimenters. We embraced a vision that a peaceful and just world was within our reach. By living that vision, we believed, we could make it a reality. It was a reality of many dimensions. We did not agree on what particulars made that vision whole. But still we lived as if that agreement was imminent in all we did. We just needed to persevere in our quest, we thought, and its undeniable truth would become self-evident.

The current reality, a fundamentally different one from what we had hoped, is not the ultimate verdict on my generation's quest. Nevertheless, it is hard to deny that a dark and prolonged interlude may be at hand. The ascendancy of the Right on a global scale is a major challenge to our generation's dreams. While it remains unclear as to the viability and staying power of rightwing populism, it is already apparent that a cornerstone of this new extremism will be the rewriting of history. We have witnessed the triumphal trope of white Christian nationalism as it marginalizes and caricaturizes so much of what our generation achieved. One need only look at the book-banning, the voter suppression, the venomous anti-muslimism and antisemitism, homophobia, and empowerment of armed citizen militias to see the potential for an ominous new world order.

This collection of essays is a modest attempt to set down in writing the lives and passions of my generation; a generation of everyday people moving through the world with hope. Some of our efforts were gravely misguided. Yet many of us, the vast majority I would like to believe, led lives that shaped, and continue to shape, a path toward a more inclusive, equitable, and sustainable future. In spite of the challenges, many of our generation indeed have persevered.

Most of the tales I have shared involve a single individual in a seemingly single-minded pursuit. Yet it would be a mistake to view these tales through the lens of present-day politics. Today such single-mindedness often accompanies an ever-more narrow identity-defined politic. Identity, of course, has been a powerful force for positive social change throughout history. Its role in Black liberation, as posited by everyone from Franz Fanon to Olúfẹ́mi Táíwò, is undeniable. But in its latter day most extreme forms, it has become increasingly reductionist, essentializing identity over all else.

The subjects of this book embraced movement-linked identities as well. But it was the norm rather than exception that civil rights activists were also anti-war activists. As the decades went by, it was also the rule that one could find these impassioned individuals graduating from one to another initiative. Civil rights activists, for obvious reasons, were a mainstay of the anti-apartheid movement, anti-war activists frequently became part of national liberation and anti-imperialist campaigns, and feminists throughout have been deeply involved in everything from human rights to union organizing.

While identity politics will likely remain a powerful force in social activism, it is not a stretch to look around us and see the potential for a renewed metanarrative not unlike that which drove my generation. The increasing sense of urgency over the transformative nature of climate change is showing signs that it may become the clarion call for a renewed generational quest. As it was for my generation, an overarching vision may once again provide a degree of synchroneity within and between current and future generations as they seek to build a better world. Likewise, it could be a global resurgence of authoritarianism, as the rise of fascism did during the second world war, that mobilizes and unites a transgenerational and multi-identity movement. It all remains to be seen. But the actions of my generation will remain touchstones if that next generational quest comes to pass.

In sharing these tales, I have been a medium as much as a subject. While these tales are based on my own journey, they are intended to be more than personal or idiosyncratic memoirs. My intention has been to cast light on larger themes, at times perhaps in the tradition of parables. Rather than make normative assertions, I have tried to leave the reader to make their own judgments. Further, we have always been a diverse bunch, my generation. So, making too fine a point of the throughlines of our lives would be both presumptive and a violation of the very essence of who we are. The selection of tales to share was of course my moment of license. While at times difficult, I find refraining from further opining or posturing a difficult but necessary coda at this late stage of my life. It is my hope that the reader will be moved to carry their interpretation of our past endeavors into their own quest in the years to come.

For now, let me conclude by way of a postscript on what I think is at the heart of all quests. Is it that which we have achieved, or is it the passion, vision, and principles with which we pursued our quest, that is the true measure of our passage through this world?

16. Postscript: In Search of the Paper Nautilus — Life is a Beach After All

I have spent endless days wandering the beaches of El Mogote on the western coast of the Sea of Cortez. With eyes downcast to avoid the sun's early morning glare, I scanned the surf line while soft waves washed across glistening sand, dying as they climbed the rising littoral before me. I have passed those hours searching for an elusive artifact, the mythical paper nautilus. I have trekked the long white strand over the better part of two decades, never finding anything greater than broken shards of the intricately crafted vessel poet Marianne Moore described as that "perishable souvenir of hope." The search for the paper nautilus has become a defining feature of my life along that little-known shore.

The paper nautilus is the common, and not entirely accepted, name of the argonaut (*Argonauta argo*), a unique species of octopus. Unlike the other roughly one hundred octopus species that dwell near the ocean's floor, the argonaut lives its entire life near the very top of the ocean's water column. It ebbs and flows with the currents, occasionally hitching rides on driftwood or jellyfish, constantly avoiding predatory fish and seabirds. The paper nautilus is crafted by the female argonaut out of calcite secreted from the tips of her tentacles. She creates a translucent and paper-thin casing (technically not a shell) ranging from several inches to more than a foot in length. When the female argonaut is ready to give birth, she lays her eggs inside the recently crafted paper nautilus, at times over one hundred thousand eggs in a single event, and then crawls in to brood her offspring. Once hatched, both tiny newborns and mother abandon the paper nautilus and swim into the warm waters near the ocean's surface. The abandoned egg casing floats on the currents, usually crushed by waves or picked apart by predators, crumbling into unidentifiable ocean detritus. But in oh-so-rare moments, a complete paper nautilus drifts ashore. Dried by the sun and winds, the translucent egg casing turns into a brittle white prize waiting to reward the persistence of only the worthiest seekers.

The paper nautilus has been wrapped in mythology since the time of the ancient Greeks. In his *History of Animals*, written around 300 B.C., Aristotle mistakenly reported that the paper nautilus-encased argonaut used its webbed tentacles as sails and rudders to navigate on ocean winds. This erroneous assumption survived for centuries and was still common among scientists throughout the nineteenth century. Jules Verne also believed the argonaut used sails to navigate the seas and in 1870 described dozens drifting on a gentle breeze in his famous novel *Twenty Thousand Leagues Under the Sea*. As the local lore of the Baja California Sur has it, the paper nautilus casts forth its offspring on the full moon. Unfortunately, there is no scientific evidence to support this claim either. More likely the stronger tides and currents caused by that same full moon bring the delicate egg cases to the shore, leading beachcombers to more frequently make their discoveries during that phase of the lunar cycle.

On my first visit to El Mogote, I met a woman from the States who lived in a small condo complex on the eastern tip of the peninsula. She regaled me one morning with a tale of her discovery of an intact paper nautilus. She was aglow, describing her find in something akin to spiritual awe. Breathlessly she explained how she now had this treasure preserved in a glass case in her home in Arizona. Her voice flush with reverence, she described her paper nautilus perched on her living-room mantel as if on a sacred altar.

With her inspiration I began my quest. Each morning, and again whenever the ebb tide occurred during daylight hours, I prowled that shoreline. I soon discovered the sea daily gave up any number of natural wonders. I found beautifully colored shells of widely varying sizes and shapes, and sand dollars with a five-petal-patterned topside and a lacy filigreed underside on a white three-inch disk. I have even found the wicked serrated spike of the Cortez stingray, a formidable weapon attached to the ray's tail to ward off predators and unsuspecting waders who inadvertently step on the otherwise docile creatures resting in the warm sands at water's edge. But never a paper nautilus.

El Mogote is a six-mile-long sandbar, about a mile and a half at its widest, which runs eastward from the Baja California Sur mainland along the northern edge of the Bay of La Paz. A mostly barren and desert-like stretch of brush and dunes, it is bordered on its southern bayside with extensive mangroves rich with sea life as described nearly eighty years ago by John Steinbeck in *The Log of the Sea of Cortez*. The peninsula creates a perfect barrier between the City of La Paz to its south and the Sea of Cortez to the north. Its eastern tip ends at the entrance to the bay where a relatively deep channel allows smaller merchant ships, fishing boats, pleasure crafts, and other seafarers access to the Sea while protecting the La Paz harbor from occasionally powerful storms.

On most mornings I would take a long slow run on the northern side of El Mogote, enjoying the sun and surf as I searched the beach. At the end of a good jog, I would walk up the sloping sands through clumps of tall grass to perch atop a dune and gaze out on the sea beyond. At times I would see huge manta rays soar high out of the water hundreds of yards out from the shore, plunging back into the sea with an explosive splash. Other times the shoreline waters close in would churn with powerful rooster fish or jacks chasing schools of smaller fish. Occasionally pods of porpoises would roll lazily through the waters no more than fifty yards from shore. After whiling away an hour or so I would walk down to firmly packed sand at the surf's edge and begin a slow jog back to the condo where I was staying. Dropping my gaze from the sunlight fracturing off the glass-smooth sea, I would search the waterline at my feet and begin again my quest for a treasure partially hidden in bleached-white sands.

Over the years I have seen the population on El Mogote grow as more condominiums, houses, a golf course, and restaurants have arrived, probably helping to explain, I tell myself, why I have yet to find my paper nautilus. The competition has grown as each morning, no matter how early I rise, I find at least one other intrepid beachcomber patrolling the surf line in that characteristic gate with shoulders hunched forward and eyes downcast.

To improve my prospects, I began venturing further north from La Paz along the peninsula's eastern coastline. First, I explored the beaches around Loreto with no better results. I took a wonderful side trip up into the Sierra de la Giganta mountains to the west of Loreto, a desolate range of rocky, barren peaks once described by Steinbeck as "the foreboding stone mountains." I drove several hours up into the mountains until I came to the magical village of San Javier. One of the oldest Spanish missions in the Americas, it was tucked into a mountainous desert that at first glance appeared bereft of life outside of occasional scrawny cows, goats, or the ubiquitous vultures circling on the updrafts from the searing desert floor. The village had a small aqueduct running through it with a steady flow of clear cool water from an unknown source, running down a nearly three-foot-wide channel bordered by 400-year-old olive trees, gnarled, and twisted but still bearing fruit.

As I ventured out into more remote areas, I came upon beautiful spring-fed pools sometimes hundreds of feet in length, surrounded by palm trees and dense foliage with small trout, tree frogs, and other creatures inhabiting the oasis. There were numerous hummingbirds flitting among the flowers, adding color and life to the hot desert air. Gradually I became aware of a wider range of birds, reptiles, and other desert dwellers where I had first assumed life largely did not exist. Still, despite its allure, the wonders of those remote stone mountains did not take me any closer to realizing my goal. I soon returned to the Sea of Cortez and my search for the paper nautilus.

To explore still further up the coastline, I borrowed a friend's jeep and headed up to the Bahía Concepción. The Sea of Cortez is considered one of the least-polluted oceans of the planet, and Bahía Concepción is perhaps the most pristine region of that Sea. It is home to many incredible creatures, large and small. It is the breeding grounds of many fish, like yellow fin tuna, yellow tail, mackerel, and other pelagic species. Bahía Concepción is also the birthing grounds of the gray whale, one of the world's largest mammals, or what biologist Paul Ehrlich referred to as "the charismatic mega-vertebrates."

I stopped for a few days in a small community of mostly expats called Posada Concepción. A chaotic mix of recreational vehicles, trailers, and several nicely constructed, ranch-style homes supported an intriguing cast of characters living mostly on a seasonal basis in a small cove adjacent to the coastal highway. I met a retired couple from Colorado who had built a cozy little home on the beach. He was a singer whose repertoire was almost entirely Frank Sinatra, and he was good. His wife was the social networker, adding the occasional visitor to their little enclave to her blog, and occasionally organizing parties to lure her connections back for a visit.

I borrowed one of their kayaks to explore further into the bay and surrounding islands. Paddling through crystal clear water I could see beautiful shells spread across the seabed some thirty feet below. At one point I saw an unusual rainbow-colored reflection off an object on the sandy bottom. I beached my kayak on one of the islands in the bay, this one little more than fifty yards across, and swam out the short distance to where I had seen the curious reflection. It was an easy dive down to the sandy spot at the edge of a patch of eel grass. I discovered that the reflection came from the open face of a sawtooth pen shell, a bivalve common to the Sea of Cortez. The shell's mother-of-pearl inner lining gave off a gorgeous opalescent sheen that glowed in the sunlight filtering from above. The shell was the largest of this species I had ever seen, well over a foot in length. I was about to ascend with my new discovery when I noticed tiny eyes protruding from the sandy seafloor near where the shell had lain. I took the shell ashore and dove back down to the seabed where I discovered an abundance of large chocolate clams, each almost the size of my hand, buried just beneath the sand. I collected a half dozen for the evening meal. A small fire on the beach to roast the clams, a bottle of hot sauce I had packed in the jeep, and an Indio, the local dark beer, made a perfect ending to a spectacular day of free diving in Bahía Concepción.

That beautiful shell was the first real treasure from my explorations of the Baja California Sur. I hoped it represented a turn in my luck as it soon made its way to my living room mantel in the States, a placeholder I told myself, for the paper nautilus.

After several more days and nights exploring Bahía Concepción, I retraced my journey to Loreto, returning the jeep to my friend, and then took the half-day bus ride further south to La Paz. The following morning, I was up early, eager to renew my search. But as soon as I reached the waterline, I saw the friendly free spirit of El Mogote who had repeatedly regaled me with the wonders of the paper nautilus. She was walking briskly up the beach, with one hand holding her sun hat canted atop her head against the morning breeze while waving to me with the other.

"So, any luck in finding a paper nautilus?" she asked with eyebrow arched inquisitively.

Like a chastened child I turned my palms upward with a shrug, "Well, I found half of one." How pathetic I felt. Still smiling brightly, she told me of a friend who had recently arrived. On his first morning he found four perfectly intact paper nautiluses on a single stroll down the beach.

My response was visceral, clearly poorly hidden as she took a step to the side, giving me a wider berth. While I did not immediately speak, I thought to myself, It seems so unjust, and after all those days scouring the ocean's edge! In thinly veiled exacerbation I asked, "Does anyone deserve to find more than one?"

She gave me a most ethereal smile and said, as if giving up on one who clearly does not understand the deeper meaning of our lives, "You know, I saw one on eBay in a glass case just like I have for only $1,500."

I gave her a thin half-smile, pivoted brusquely, and began jogging down the beach. I could barely hold back the urge to shout, That is just so damned unfair! The slow morning run was about to turn into a long hard sprint.

The next day I decided to take my snorkeling gear in a backpack to explore the waters off a more isolated stretch further up the peninsula. It was a cooler day, so I had delayed my run until midafternoon. A couple of miles up the beach I stopped and put on my mask and fins. I plunged into the sea, hoping it would curb the disappointment of yet another day's search left empty-handed. As I swam outward, I thought to myself, My luck must change one of these days. My quest cannot go unrequited forever, can it? Soon I was lost in the warm clear waters far from any sign of beachcombers or other terrestrial-bound creatures. The bottom sloped gradually away from the shore and was mostly sea grass and sand which meant there was far less sea life than I had hoped. But the water temperature was luxuriously warm, and I let the easy draw of the ebb tide carry me out to sea.

I began following a school of small silvery fish that made flashing sharp turns in unison when I dove down amongst them, as if they were of a single mind. They settled into a comfortable distance fifteen yards ahead of me as we swam just above the seafloor in roughly twenty feet of water.

I was not really paying attention to where we were headed as I repeatedly dove down to follow the school until I soon found myself well over one hundred yards out from shore. The water was still only about thirty feet deep, and I could see for quite a distance. Then the fish vanished in an instant leaving me staring into an empty abyss that darkened at the far edge of my vision. It was as if the sea had emptied in the blink of an eye. Upon resurfacing I heard someone make a loud sharp whistle. I looked up. Ahead of me, another fifty yards out to sea, was a man standing in an open skiff, a twenty-foot launch called a *panga.* He was one of the calamari fishermen preparing his gear for a night's fishing further out on the sea. He waved his arms urgently over his head to capture my attention. Then with one arm he pointed emphatically to my left. About halfway between us and off to the north another fifty yards was a massive fin cutting through the smooth calm sea. The fin was as big as a car door. For a moment I just froze, not moving, not breathing. I then ducked my head under the water and watched a huge creature, its massive tail gliding slowly from side to side as it swam steadily toward me. It was easily twenty feet long with its mouth open wide, a gaping maw nearly as wide as the spread of my outstretched arms. It was a moment reminiscent of Samuel Johnson's famous observation (paraphrased)—*There is nothing quite like a hanging to so wonderfully focus the mind.*

Wonderful or otherwise, my mind was indeed focused like nothing I could recall. No thoughts of a failed quest, of an aggravatingly blissful beachcomber, not even of a paper nautilus. My entire being was entranced by that massive presence bearing down on me, now only ten yards away. And then I suddenly realized what was upon me, and I exhaled as if I had been holding my breath for an eternity. It was a whale shark, the largest fish in the sea, roughly the size of the fishing boat now behind it. It was a juvenile no less. The adult whale shark reaches fifty feet, the size of a full-length school bus. It swam ever so slowly alongside me. A big, flat head and spots all along its body, I could have reached out and touched it as it eased to one side of me. I began to relax as I quickly remembered that whale sharks are plankton eaters, not snorkeler eaters. Its large unblinking eye studied me as it eased past. Whale sharks swim or just drift along with the currents for hours on end with their gaping mouths seining great quantities of plankton from near the ocean's surface.

I settled in and began swimming next to this beautiful, docile behemoth. We moved in slow tandem for what seemed like hours but probably was only twenty or thirty minutes. I lost track of time before noticing the light fading around us as the sun began to settle in the west. I was still one hundred yards from shore and decided now was the time to abandon my reverie with this most magical of ocean dwellers. Soon the sea life would begin to change as the creatures of the dark, some of them not nearly so docile, would arrive at their evening feeding grounds. To further emphasize the point, I remembered that Guadalupe Island was just across the isthmus on the Pacific side of the Baja. Guadalupe is a breeding ground of the great white shark that occasionally ventures into the Sea of Cortez. They can grow to nearly the size of that juvenile whale shark, but I am happy to say I have never had the pleasure of an encounter.

Whale Shark in the Sea of Cortez

With reluctance I broke off my drift with the young whale shark and swam back to shore. As I waded in from the surf the adrenalin that had surged through me over the past hour gradually gave way to a sense of serenity and the odd sensation that a great burden had been lifted from me. As I began the long slow walk back it occurred to me that I might encounter that ever-present beachcombing woman who seemed to be waiting whenever I returned from an unsuccessful hunt for the paper nautilus. Yet this time the prospects of another inquisition did not lead to disquietude but instead provoked a slight smile. She really was quite nice, I thought, in her own quirky way.

Looking out across the Sea of Cortez, I watched the gradual shifting of colors in the evening sky as the late afternoon gave way to the coming dusk. The calamari fishermen were arriving to their nightly fishing stations out on the open sea and beginning to light their lanterns to attract squid and various other fish to their lines. The lanterned fishing boats were rising and falling on gently rolling waves, disappearing into a trough only to reappear moments later atop the swell, looking ever so much like a string of blinking Christmas lights strung along the horizon, as peaceful a sunset as I had ever seen.

The exhilaration of the afternoon was evolving into a sense of reverence as the world around me softly changed. As dusk descended, I pondered the wonderful day just coming to an end as one is wont to do in such moments, and then reflected further back upon the many other wonderful days over the years of my sojourn. I asked myself, So who is to say my luck needs to turn? Maybe I am already the luckiest man alive.

One's quest will always come to an end, whether in a moment's encounter with a great leviathan of the deep, or in the quiet grasp of unrelenting age. It is the quest that speaks to our passage through this world, the achievements mere signposts along the journey. While not diminishing the goals, I came to accept it is that to which we devote ourselves that is our essence. The goals will remain elusive, but how we pursue them will define us.

With my shoulders more squared, I cast my gaze not to the sand at my feet nor along the wave's edge as it slid up the beach in assault of the unmoving dunes, but toward the dying light in the evening sky. I walked slowly but purposely back the way I had come only hours past, relishing the colors of the sunset as it played across the sweeping canvas of the Sea of Cortez. Perhaps tomorrow, a new quest awaits, with new challenges, new joys, and new lessons to be learned.

Life is a journey
Not a destination

Ralph Waldo Emerson

Credits

Prelude to a Quest

A Time of Awakening

"Chicago," by Graham Nash (Nash Notes/Nash Music LLC), quoted with permission from The Mark Spector Company.

The Better Angels of Our Nature

Cover photo – Courtesy *The Napa Valley Register* – with permission from Managing Editor Dan Evans
Motorcycle photos – Courtesy of Juvinall family collection, permission - Jacqueline Zwick.

Scouts Honor and the Vietnam War

Cover photo – author's private collection

Lil Sis and the Women's Health Movement

Cover by Betty Szudy, with permission.

When Martha Graham Crashed Fight Night

Cover photo by Robert Przybysz – with permission

Days of the Commune

Cover Photo – Courtesy *The Napa Register*, managing editor Dan Evans.
Photo end of chapter – Courtesy of photographer Ron Kyle

The Brigade

Cover photo – Courtesy of AP photo

A Time of Revolution: The Nicaragua Years

Gladys and Noel: A Love Story

All photos Courtesy of Bolt family collection.

El Poeta

Cover photo: public domain.

I Can't Just Leave

Cover photo – "Community," by Thelma Gomez and Freddy Gaitán, courtesy of Casa Ben Linder
Photo of Ben and colleague at micro dam Courtesy of Mira Brown.

Free Diving With Guido

Cover photo – By Agile LeVin – with permission

Everyday People, Extraordinary Lives

Connie Stay Home for Peace

All photos courtesy of Bob Fitch Photography Archive, Department of Special Collections, Stanford University Library, except Peace Boyz photo, courtesy of photographer Norm Bleier.

That's the Guy

Cover photo – with permission, Reuters News Agency Photo of Bob Thomson – provided by Thomson with permission.

By Any Other Name

Cover photo with permission - Byrd Williams Family Photography Collection, University of North Texas Special Collections.

A Long Road to Justice

Cover photo – By Harry Mattison, with permission.

The Blessing

Cover photo – Courtesy of Allison Otu, Executive Director of Marketing and Communications, The Walter Cronkite School of Journalism and Mass Media.

The Quest Continues

Postscript: The Search for the Paper Nautilus—Life is a Beach After All

Cover Photo – Courtesy of photographer Jason Stonhewer. Photo of Whale Shark – Licensed through Bigstock.com.

Douglas L. Murray is Professor Emeritus, Department of Sociology, Colorado State University.

https://sociology.colostate.edu/people/wpmurrayd

www.ingramcontent.com/pod-product-compliance
Lightning Source LLC
LaVergne TN
LVHW020510100826
845148LV00003B/743
9781628802771